Everyday Baking with Chef Brad

"America's Grain Guy"

Brad E Petersen

Changing the world one grain at a time

Ralph McKnight Publishing
Mapleton, Utah

Everyday Baking with Chef Brad
Special Full-Color Edition

© 2017 by Brad E Petersen
All rights reserved. No part of this work
covered by copyright may be
used, reproduced, stored in a retrieval
system, or transmitted in any form or by
any means, electronic, mechanical, photocopying,
recording, or otherwise without the prior written
permission of the copyright holder, except brief
quotations used in a review.

Notice: The purpose of this book is to educate and
entertain. The author and Ralph McKnight
Publishing shall have neither liability nor
responsibility to any person or entity with
respect to any loss or damage caused, or
alleged to have been caused, directly or
indirectly, by the information contained in this
book.

Special Full-Color Edition published 2017

ISBN: 978-1546931096

Photography: Louise Petersen, Mulberry Corner Photography
Cover design and layout: Marianne McKnight

For any questions about recipes, including grains
and other ingredients, check Chef Brad's website:
www.chefbrad.com
or email chef@chefbrad.com

Chef Brad's World: www.chefbrad.com

Acknowledgments

This book has become a labor of love. I love baking and I have seen the need for healthful baked goods that still taste great and are a joy to eat. I have also seen the need in our current culture for healthful gluten-free recipes.

I worked for one year in a gluten-free bakery and I learned a lot — mostly, about what not to do in creating gluten-free food. I gained 25 pounds while working in this bakery. I loved the cakes and pastries, but they were packed with sugars and simple carbs. I really tried to influence the owners to use whole grains but to no avail. I am grateful for the time spent at that bakery; I left with a desire to create healthful, grain-filled, gluten-free pastries and baked goods.

When I was planning this cookbook, however, I didn't want to lock myself into featuring exclusively gluten-free recipes. I decided to create a book that offered everything — Whole Grain, Wheat Free, and Gluten Free. I had so much fun creating these recipes. With the addition of video links, this book is unique. With *Everyday Baking with Chef Brad*, you will be able to create great baked goods — gluten free or not — for your families. We all know someone who is gluten free, and oftentimes we stress about how to prepare food for them. No worries now; the recipes in this book will fill your needs — from breads to breakfast foods, from cookies to burger buns. You will love this book.

This is my first full-color cookbook. I was trying to do it on my own, with limited success. There was so much to cook and to photograph. My lovely wife, Louise, fortunately stepped in and took over the photography for me. It could not have been better. She is amazing and has an eye for detail. We loved working together on this book, so much so that we are already planning the next cookbook.

Perhaps one of the most essential parts of creating a cookbook is the publisher. My publishers, Ralph and Marianne McKnight, are outstanding — detailed to the max and so patient with me on every account. They actually have been with me from the beginning, through all the ups and downs, always willing to jump in and make it happen.

Whole grains are amazing. I love them — especially for their versatility. Grains contain optimal nutrients for the body, along with fiber, minerals, and essential fatty acids. In a world where our food is devoid of these things, we need to know how to cook with these wonderful grains. *Everyday Baking with Chef Brad* fits the bill. If you have any questions, you can contact me at chef@chefbrad.com. Enjoy the journey!

Chef Brad
"America's Grain Guy"

Dedication

This book is dedicated to everyone who has supported me over the years and everyone who has encouraged me to continue pursuing my passion, even when it looked hopeless at times. I have learned that staying true to our passion, no matter what, is perhaps one of the most important things we can ever do.

Contents

Meet Chef Brad

Introduction 1

About WonderFlour™ 3

Recipes

    Breads 4

    Cakes 46

    Cookies & Crackers 62

    Pancakes & Waffles 86

    Muffins & Biscuits 102

Polish Stoneware 122

Index 123

Resources

    Ongoing Education – Cooking Videos by Chef Brad 125

    Quality Equipment for Quality Baking 126

Meet Chef Brad

Chef Brad, known as "America's Grain Guy" is a leading authority in the use of grains in America. Chef Brad has established a following in the Baking World, as well as with the Health and Wellness World. Now with this cookbook he will make a stand in the Gluten-Free/Wheat-Free/Whole-Grain Baking World. Chef Brad has proved time and time again that Healthy can taste great without compromising taste or texture.

In Chef Brad's spare time, he travels nation-wide sharing his love and passion for grain and food. His Chef Brad Events are highly sought after and his online Health and Wellness Program, called "The Revolution," is quickly becoming one of the top health and wellness programs in the country.

Chef Brad lives in sunny Arizona with his wife of over 30 years. He enjoys time spent with his five children and ever-growing population of grandchildren. Chef Brad loves gardening, baking, making gourmet ice cream, and brewing Kombucha.

Video: Who is Chef Brad?

Introduction

I am happy to present *Everyday Baking with Chef Brad*. It is unique in so many ways. The recipes in this cookbook are almost all whole grain and include gluten-free and wheat-free alternatives. Gluten-free baked goods can be great tasting, healthful, and enjoyable to prepare. There is a lot of gluten-free garbage out there, and we have learned to not like it. Not only that, we are told not to eat grains and, in the process, are losing our battle on health and wellness. This book is designed to change your opinion of whole grains and gluten-free food.

Look for this **GF** symbol for gluten-free recipes and tips.

You will notice QR Codes on some of the recipes, as well as in the back of the book. Scanning these codes on an imaging device, such as some phones, will link you to some of my instructional videos. These videos are designed to enhance your baking experience. Some offer baking helps, while others feature variations of some of the recipes in this book. While the ingredients may vary, the techniques will hopefully be useful to you as you embark into what is perhaps a whole new world for you — the world of baking, gluten-free baking in particular.

Gluten-free baking does not have to be hard. In fact, one thing I always tell my students is: "If you are stressing during the baking process, you are doing something wrong." Baking should be relaxing and enjoyable as you contemplate the joy of the finished product. Don't be afraid to try new things and, by all means, have fun along the way! If you have questions, feel free to contact me at chef@chefbrad.com.

There are a couple of things I have learned over the years that can help you gain confidence in the kitchen. At the top of the list is this: Use quality ingredients and quality equipment to get the job done. Quality ingredients simply mean clean, chemical-free, natural ingredients that assure success in your baking — and, even more importantly, add value to your health and wellness.

What I know about quality equipment has come from years of learning the hard way. When things don't turn out right, most often it can be the result of the equipment. When we constantly burn or over-cook, that is the time to upgrade to better pans for baking. I recommend USA Pans. I love them and have used them for years. USA Pans generously donated the pans used in the production of this cookbook. You will also notice the stoneware in the photographs. I love using Polish stoneware, not only for its beauty but for how functional it is. Everything I bake in it turns out great.

Of course, to bake with whole grains, you need a good quality mill and mixer. For health and wellness — and just for everyday baking — you need a good grain mill to grind the grains fresh and a good mixer to mix the breads and baked goods without difficulty. I absolutely adore the WonderMill and WonderMix — proven beyond measure to be quality in every respect.

Everyday Baking with Chef Brad has just about everything you might need for quality baking in your home. I have tried to make the recipes easy to follow and have included recipes that I hope you will love and want to bake again and again. Each recipe either comes with a companion gluten-free version or simple tips on how to adapt it to gluten free. My hope is to help you feed those you love, regardless of gluten restrictions.

I have left space on some of the pages for you to jot down notes about your baking experiences. What grain combinations did you try and like? Which grains didn't you care for? What variations did you incorporate? Include other notes-to-self.

Just one more comment about this book. When it comes to gluten-free, wheat-free baking, I have found the secret to success is using a combination of grains, blended to create a more complete flour for baking. I share my WonderFlour™ formula on grinding your own fabulous whole-grain flours on the next page. I've had great success with this formula and have taught it for years, with great feedback.

Trust the process and enjoy the journey!

About WonderFlour™

I have been working on my WonderFlour™ formula for years, perfecting the process. I am happy to share my this formula with you, because I know that it will enhance the nutrient value and flavor of the foods you create. You can also purchase my WonderFlour™ and Gluten-Free WonderFlour™ blends. Go to my website, www.chefbrad.com, for more information.

WonderFlour™ is a blend of three or more wheat-free grains. WonderFlour™ can take the place of white flour in almost all of your baking and cooking. In fact, the only kind of baking in which you shouldn't use WonderFlour™ is in yeasted breads — WonderFlour™ doesn't have sufficient gluten. You can use WonderFlour™ with confidence in everything else, however. It really is a wonderful, healthful, all-purpose flour.

To Make WonderFlour™:

1. Measure equal parts of three or more whole grains into a large bowl and mix well. One of my favorite combinations is spelt, pearled barley, and brown rice.

2. Grind the blend of grains in your WonderMill — the breads setting for breads, pastry setting for cakes and cookies, and coarse setting for corn.

It's as simple as that!

> To make Gluten-Free WonderFlour™, simply use a blend of three or more gluten-free grains — your choice.

To Use WonderFlour™:

While it's best to use freshly ground flour, that isn't always convenient. When I grind my WonderFlour™, I like to do enough to fill a large bucket that I can seal. I place the bucket in my pantry, where it is readily available for me to use in all of my baking. Don't stress about how long WonderFlour™ can be stored. At its worse, this whole-grain flour is far better than the low-quality white flour you buy in stores. When measuring, use WonderFlour™ cup for cup for the flour amount in recipes.

I hope you love WonderFlour™ as much as I do. I wish you the greatest success in all your culinary adventures.

Video: Healthy Gluten-Free Flour

Basic Whole-Wheat Bread

This bread can be 100% whole wheat, but Natural White flour really adds to the texture and overall end result of the bread.

Natural White flour, produced by Wheat Montana, is an all-purpose flour that is unbleached and unbromated, which means it is free of potassium bromate, a toxin found in many commercial flours.

Ingredients

4 cups hot water
1/3 cup canola oil
1/2 cup honey
3 tablespoons sugar
1 tablespoon salt
8 to 10 cups hard white wheat flour, or red wheat, freshly ground
1/4 cup instant yeast
2 to 4 cups Natural White flour (optional)

Yield: 3 loaves

Directions

1. In WonderMix bowl, with dough hook, place water, oil, sweetener, and salt.
2. Add 8 cups of whole-grain flour on top of ingredients.
3. Place yeast on top of whole-grain flour.
4. Turn on mixer and add more flour, including Natural White flour, until dough pulls away from sides of bowl.
5. Knead for 6 minutes.
6. Before turning off mixer, drizzle oil around dough to help it come out of bowl.
7. Turn off mixer and remove dough, placing it on an oiled counter top.
8. Form dough into 2-pound loaves and place in bread pans.
9. Let rise, covered with light cloth, until double in size, about 20 to 25 minutes.
10. While dough is rising, preheat oven to 400°F.
11. Place in oven, immediately lowering temperature to 350°F, and bake for 25 to 30 minutes, or until internal temperature is 180°F.
12. Remove from oven, remove from pans, and let cool.

Video: Homemade Wheat Bread

Breads 7

Whole-Grain Gluten-Free Bread

Ingredients

6 eggs
2 cups hot water
2/3 cup cooking oil
1/2 cup honey
1 tablespoon balsamic vinegar
6 cups gluten-free flour
2 teaspoons salt
2 tablespoons xanthan gum
1 cup potato starch
1 1/2 cups flax meal
1 cup gluten-free cracked cereal blend)
3 tablespoons instant yeast

Yield: 2 loaves

Directions

1. In WonderMix bowl, with French whips, place eggs, water, oil, honey, and vinegar.
2. Whip well.
3. Remove whips and replace with dough hook.
4. In separate bowl, sift together flour, salt, xanthan gum, potato starch, flax meal, cracked grains, and yeast.
5. With mixer turned on, add flour mixture and mix for 6 minutes.
6. Turn off mixer and scoop dough into 2 bread pans, partially lined with parchment paper. The parchment should run the length of the pan and over the ends.
7. Smooth dough with wet fingers.
8. Place in a warm area and let rise to double.
9. While dough is rising, preheat oven to 400°F.
10. Place in oven, immediately lowering temperature to 350°F, and bake for 25 to 30 minutes, or until internal temperature is 180°F.
11. Remove from oven and let cool slightly. You may need to use a knife to loosen sides of loaves. Hold on to ends of parchment paper and lift out loaf.

Nothing is better than the smell — and taste — of a loaf of homemade bread, hot out of the oven. With the Chef Brad method, you can now enjoy freshly baked gluten-free bread at home.

Do not spray pans for gluten-free breads.

The problem with most gluten-free baked goods is the huge amounts of sugar and over-processed ingredients that are used to produce products that are edible. Gluten-free can be just as good without all the garbage. Simple whole grains and quality ingredients are the secret to preparing all good foods — that applies to gluten-free also.

Video: Easy Gluten-Free Bread

Whole-Wheat Flax Sourdough Bread

Soaking the flax seed brings out the rich, nutty flavor of the grain.

Ingredients

- 1 cup sourdough starter
- 2 cups hot water
- 1/4 cup organic agave
- 1/2 cup flax seeds, soaked (this replaces the oil)
- 2 teaspoons salt
- 2 cups hard red wheat, hard white wheat, or spelt flour, freshly ground
- 3 tablespoons instant yeast
- 3 to 4 cups Natural White flour

Yield: 1 large freestanding loaf or 2 small loaves

My goal is to cut out the majority of white sugar and white flour from my diet. I do use white flour but only when there is yeast in the recipe — and then I only use chemical-clean, good-quality flours.

Directions

1. Make sure you soak the flax seeds — especially for this recipe.
2. In WonderMix bowl, using dough hook, place sourdough, water, agave, flax seeds, salt, and freshly ground flour. Place yeast on top.
3. Turn on mixer, adding white flour until dough pulls away from sides of bowl.
4. Mix for 5 to 6 minutes.
5. Remove dough from mixer.
6. Divide dough into 2 parts. Form into freestanding loaves and place on parchment paper.
7. Let rise until double.
8. While dough is rising, preheat oven and pizza stone to 400°F.
9. Bake on pizza stone for 30 to 40 minutes.

Soak flax seed overnight, using a 2 to 1 ration: 2 parts water to 1 part seeds. Soaking flax brings out the natural fats and flavor. Flax has an amazing flavor and adds great fiber to breads, not to mention texture and beauty.

Video: Sourdough Starter

Breads 9

Gluten-Free Flax Bread

Ingredients

6 eggs
2 cups hot water
2/3 cup cooking oil
1/2 cup organic agave
1 tablespoon balsamic vinegar
7 cups gluten-free flour
2 teaspoons salt
2 tablespoons xanthan gum
1 cup potato starch
1 1/2 cups flax meal
1/4 cup yeast

Yield: 1 large freestanding loaf or 2 small loaves

Directions

1. In WonderMix bowl, with French whips, place eggs, water, oil, agave, and vinegar.
2. Whip well.
3. In separate bowl, sift together flour, salt, xanthan gum, potato starch, flax meal, and yeast.
4. Replace whips with dough hook. Add flour mixture and mix for 6 minutes.
5. Turn off mixer then scoop dough into 2 bread pans, partially lined with parchment paper. The parchment should run the length of the pan and over the ends.
6. Smooth dough with wet fingers.
7. Place in a warm area and let rise to double.
8. While dough is rising, preheat oven to 400°F.
9. Place in oven, immediately lowering temperature to 350°F, and bake for 25 to 30 minutes, or until internal temperature is 180°F.
10. Remove from oven and let cool slightly. You may need to use a knife to loosen sides of loaves. Hold on to ends of parchment paper and lift out loaf.

Baking a variety of breads is important to nutrition — and to the taste experience.

Grind your gluten-free grains fresh in your WonderMill. A blend of three or more grains work well. Some of my favorite grains to use are brown rice, quinoa, amaranth, sorghum, teff, and buckwheat.

Video: Easy Gluten-Free Bread

Breads

Buckwheat Rustic Bread

There is nothing better than buckwheat flour to make a bread rustic and oh so flavorful. I love the look and taste it adds to the bread.

Ingredients

- 3 eggs
- 2 cups warm milk
- 1/4 cup cooking oil
- 1/4 cup organic agave
- 1 cup sourdough starter
- 1 cup cocoa nibs
- 2 teaspoons salt
- 1 cup buckwheat flour, freshly ground
- 4 to 6 cups Natural White flour
- 3 tablespoons instant yeast
- Melted butter, for dipping

Yield: 1 large freestanding loaf or 2 small loaves

Directions

1. In WonderMix bowl, with dough hook, place eggs, milk, oil, agave, sourdough starter, cocoa nibs, salt, all the buckwheat flour, and 1 cup of the white flour. Put yeast on top.

2. Begin mixing, adding white flour until dough pulls away from sides of bowl. Do not add in all the white flour if dough pulls away before it's all added.

3. Knead for an additional 6 minutes.

4. Rub some oil on counter and remove dough from mixer.

5. Divide into 2 loaves and let rise to double.

6. While dough is rising, preheat oven to 400°F.

7. Place in oven, immediately lowering temperature to 350°F, and bake for 25 to 30 minutes, until golden brown.

To Make Dinner Rolls:

After step 4, divide the dough into pieces to form dinner rolls. Dip roll into melted butter and place on baking sheet, making sure the rolls have space between them to grow.

Grinding the whole black buckwheat at home gives you a completely different experience in texture and taste.

The objective of using whole grains is to add nutrition without compromising flavor or texture. Whole-grain foods can, and should, be packed with flavor and goodness, giving you the added benefit of fiber and nutrition.

Video: Sourdough Starter

Flax Seed Rustic Bread

There is nothing better than flax seed to make a bread rustic and flavorful. I love the look and taste it adds to the bread.

Ingredients

- 2 cups warm water
- 1/4 cup extra virgin olive oil
- 1/4 cup organic agave
- 1 cup sourdough starter
- 1 cup flax seeds, soaked overnight in 2 cups water
- 2 teaspoons salt
- 2 cups spelt flour, freshly ground
- 4 to 6 cups Natural White flour
- 2 tablespoons instant yeast

Yield: 2 freestanding loaves

Directions

1. In WonderMix bowl, with dough hook, place water, oil, agave, sourdough starter, flax, salt, all the spelt flour, 1 cup of white flour, and yeast on top.

2. Begin mixing, adding white flour until dough pulls away from sides of bowl. Do not add in all the white flour if dough pulls away before it's all added.

3. Knead for 6 minutes.

4. Rub some oil on counter and place dough on it.

5. Cut dough in half and form 2 round, freestanding loaves.

6. Place loaves on parchment paper and let rise to double.

7. While dough is rising, preheat oven and pizza stone to 400°F.

8. Place in oven, immediately lowering temperature to 350°F, and bake for 25 to 30 minutes, or until internal temperature is 180°F.

Video: Sourdough Starter

Gluten-Free Rustic Flat Bread

Ingredients

6 eggs
2 cups hot water
1/3 cup cooking oil
1/2 cup honey
1 tablespoon balsamic vinegar
1 cup flax seeds, soaked in 2 cups of water for at least 1 hour
7 cups gluten-free flour, freshly ground
2 teaspoons salt
2 tablespoons xanthan gum
1 cup potato starch
1 cup flax meal
1/4 cup instant yeast

Yield: 2 loaves

Gluten-free flour can be healthful and taste great!

Directions

1. In your WonderMix, with dough hook, place eggs, water, oil, honey, vinegar, and flax seeds.
2. Whip well.
3. In separate bowl, sift together flour, salt, xanthan gum, potato starch, flax meal, and yeast.
4. Turn on mixer and add flour mixture.
5. Mix for 6 minutes.
6. Turn off mixer then scoop dough into 2 bread pans, partially lined with parchment paper. The parchment should run the length of the pan and over the ends.
7. Smooth dough with wet fingers.
8. Place in a warm area and let rise to double.
9. While dough is rising, preheat oven to 400°F.
10. Place in oven, immediately lowering temperature to 350°F, and bake for 25 minutes, or until internal temperature is 180°F.
11. Remove from oven and let cool slightly. You may need to use a knife to loosen sides of loaves. Hold on to ends of parchment paper and lift out loaf.

The flax makes this bread nutty and addictive.

Gluten-free grains include all varieties of rice, sorghum, teff (brown and golden), amaranth, millet, kaniwa, quinoa (red, black, and white), buckwheat (whole, hulled, and roasted — kasha), corn, popcorn, finger millet (Ragi), Job's tears, and chia. While oats don't contain gluten, they are often grown next to gluten grains, like wheat and barley. You can, however, buy gluten-free oats.

Video: Gluten-Free All-Purpose Dough

Red Rice Chia Bread

The cooked red rice is amazing in this bread — nutty and lovely. This bread is a winner.

Ingredients

- 4 cups hot water
- 1/3 cup cooking oil
- 2/3 cup organic agave
- 1 cup red rice, cooked
- 1/2 cup chia seeds
- 1/2 cup cocoa nibs (optional)
- 1 tablespoon salt
- 3 cups spelt flour, freshly ground
- 3 tablespoons instant yeast
- 8 (or more) cups Natural White flour

Yield: 1 large freestanding loaf or 2 small loaves

Directions

1. In WonderMix bowl, with dough hook, place water, oil, agave, rice, chia, cocoa nibs (optional), salt, and spelt flour. Put yeast on top.
2. Turn on mixer, adding white flour until dough pulls away from sides of bowl.
3. Knead for 6 minutes.
4. Remove from bowl and divide into loaves.
5. Place in pans and let rise until double.
6. While dough is rising, preheat oven to 400°F.
7. Place in oven, immediately lowering temperature to 350°F, and bake until golden brown, or until internal temperature is 180°F.

Notes . . .

Video: Potato Bread

Gluten-Free Red Rice Chia Bread

Ingredients

6 eggs
1 cup red rice, cooked
2 cups hot water
2/3 cup cooking oil
1/2 cup organic agave
1 tablespoon balsamic vinegar
6 cups gluten-free flour, freshly ground
2 teaspoons salt
2 tablespoons xanthan gum
1 cup potato starch
1/3 cup chia seeds
1 cup cocoa nibs (optional)
4 tablespoons instant yeast
1 cup golden raisins

Yield: 2 loaves

Directions

1. In WonderMix bowl, with dough hook, place eggs, cooked rice, water, oil, agave, and vinegar.

2. Whip well.

3. In separate bowl, sift together flour, salt, xanthan gum, potato starch, chia, cocoa nibs, and yeast.

4. Turn on mixer. Add flour mixture and raisins.

5. Mix for 6 minutes.

6. Turn off mixer then scoop dough into 2 bread pans, partially lined with parchment paper. The parchment should run the length of the pan and over the ends.

7. Smooth dough with wet fingers.

8. Place in warm area and let rise to double.

9. While dough is rising, preheat oven to 400°F.

10. Place in oven, immediately lowering temperature to 350°F, and bake for 25 minutes, or until internal temperature is 180°F.

11. Remove from oven and let cool slightly. You may need to use a knife to loosen sides of loaves. Hold on to ends of parchment paper and lift out loaf.

Gluten-free breads can be as fun and exciting as your imagination will allow. Cocoa nibs add a wonderful, crunchy, chocolatey flavor.

Use a blend of three or more gluten-free grains, freshly ground.

Video: Easy Gluten-Free Bread

Multi-Grain Focaccia Bread

Using coarse kosher salt on focaccia bread is the best option.

Ingredients

- 1 1/2 cups hot water
- 1 cup sourdough starter
- 3 tablespoons sugar
- 1 tablespoon salt
- 3 tablespoons extra virgin olive oil
- 1/2 cup whole teff
- 2 cups spelt, freshly ground
- 3 tablespoons instant yeast
- 1 to 2 cups high-gluten white flour
- **Toppings:** Olive oil, coarse kosher salt, and chopped rosemary

Yield: 2 large loaves

Directions

1. In WonderMix bowl, with dough hook, place all ingredients, except high-gluten white flour, with yeast on top.
2. Turn on mixer, adding high-gluten white flour until dough cleans sides of bowl.
3. Let knead for 6 minutes.
4. Remove dough and let rise until double.
5. Punch down dough and roll out.
6. Place on parchment-lined pizza paddle and let rise.
7. While dough is rising, preheat oven and pizza stone to 500°F.
8. Punch finger holes in dough.
9. Pour olive oil over dough, brushing until covered.
10. Sprinkle with kosher salt and chopped rosemary.
11. Bake on pizza stone for 5 to 7 minutes, or until golden brown.

Notes...

Video: Sourdough Starter

Gluten-Free Rosemary Focaccia Bread

Ingredients

5 eggs
1 1/2 cups warm water
1/2 cup potato starch
1/4 cup extra virgin olive oil
1/3 cup organic agave
1 tablespoon salt
4 teaspoons xanthan gum
1/2 cup popcorn, freshly ground
4 cups gluten-free flour, freshly ground
4 tablespoons instant yeast
Toppings: Olive oil, coarse kosher salt, and chopped rosemary

Yield: 2 loaves

This bread is perfect for dipping in oil and vinegar.

Directions

1. In WonderMix bowl, with dough hook, place ingredients, with yeast on top.
2. Mix well for 2 minutes. This dough should be more like heavy cake batter rather than bread dough.
3. In large jelly roll pan, drizzle with olive oil.
4. Place scoops of dough on large piece of parchment paper, sprinkled with gluten-free flour.
5. Pat dough down to create an inch-thick dough that covers pan.
6. Drizzle with olive oil, then sprinkle with freshly chopped rosemary and kosher salt.
7. Let rise to double, about 20 minutes.
8. While dough is rising, preheat oven to 400°F.
9. Bake for 15 to 20 minutes, or until golden brown.

Topping with fresh rosemary is delightful!

Grind your gluten-free grains fresh in your WonderMill. A blend of three or more grains work well. I like to use a combination of brown rice, quinoa, amaranth, sorghum, teff, or buckwheat.

Be patient and let the bread rise before baking. It does take a while.

Video: Gluten-Free All-Purpose Dough

Teff Pizza Dough

Teff in pizza dough is amazing and works well. It adds a crispy texture that everyone loves. Just use the whole grain. Amaranth and chia seeds also work well in pizza dough.

Ingredients

- 1 cup sourdough starter
- 1 1/2 cups hot water, or 1 bottle hard cider or beer
- 3 tablespoon extra virgin olive oil
- 3 tablespoons organic agave
- 1 cup whole teff, uncooked
- 2 teaspoons salt
- 3 (or more) cups Natural White flour
- 2 tablespoons instant yeast

Yield: 3 to 6 pizzas, depending on size and thickness

Directions

1. In WonderMix bowl, with dough hook, place sourdough starter, liquid, teff, salt, and 3 cups of flour, placing yeast on top. Turn on mixer.
2. Mix, adding more flour until dough pulls away from sides of bowl.
3. Knead for 6 minutes.
4. Remove from mixer and let rise.
5. While dough is rising, preheat oven and pizza stone to 500°F.
6. Divide dough into 2 or 3 pieces, depending on size of pizza you want.
7. Roll out dough into a circle to desired thickness. Place on parchment paper.
8. Top with desired toppings.
9. Using pizza paddle or flat cookie sheet, place pizza into hot, preheated pizza stone and bake 5 to 7 minutes, or until desired doneness.
10. Remove from oven and start with next pizza.

Preparing pizza on parchment paper and baking on a pizza stone greatly enhances the pizza experience.

Notes . . .

Video: Sourdough Starter

Gluten-Free Pizza Dough

Ingredients

5 eggs
1 1/2 cups warm water
1/4 cup extra virgin olive oil
1/2 cup potato starch
1/4 cup sugar
4 cups gluten-free flour, freshly ground on pastry setting (reserve 1/2 cup flour for making pizzas)
1 tablespoon salt
4 teaspoons xanthan gum
2 tablespoons instant yeast

Yield: 3 to 6 pizzas, depending on size and thickness

Directions

1. Preheat oven to 500°F if baking on a pizza stone or 400°F if baking on a pan.
2. In WonderMix bowl, with dough hook, place ingredients, with yeast on top.
3. Mix well for 2 minutes. This dough should be more like heavy cake batter rather than bread dough.
4. Scoop desired amount of dough on to parchment paper, sprinkled with gluten-free flour.
5. Sprinkle dough with gluten-free flour and pat down into a circle.
6. Top with desired toppings, leaving dough on parchment paper.
7. Bake either on pizza stone or on a pan until done.

Every time I make this recipe, I like it more and more, and I think why is because I get more comfortable with it and more creative. I like pre-baking the pizzas and having them on hand in the freezer.

Watch Chef Brad's video on Delicious Gluten-Free Pizza by scanning the QR Code below.

Notes . . .

Video: Delicious Gluten-Free Pizza

Flax Dinner Rolls

Soaking the flax really brings out the nutty flavor of the flax seeds.

Ingredients

2 eggs
2 cups warm milk
1/2 cup flax seeds, soaked in 1 cup of water for at least 1 hour
1/4 cup organic agave
1 cup sourdough starter
2 teaspoons salt
2 cups spelt flour, freshly ground
4 to 6 cups Natural White flour
3 tablespoons instant yeast
Butter, melted, for dipping

Yield: 2 dozen

Directions

1. In WonderMix bowl, with dough hook, place eggs, milk, flax, agave, sourdough starter, salt, all of the spelt flour, and 1 cup of the white flour. Place yeast on top.

2. Begin mixing, adding white flour until dough pulls from sides of bowl. Do not add in all the white flour if dough pulls away before it's all added.

3. Once dough pulls from sides, knead for 6 minutes.

4. Rub some oil on counter and remove dough from mixer.

5. With your hands, divide dough into pieces to form dinner rolls.

6. Dip each roll into melted butter and place on baking sheet, making sure rolls have space between to grow.

7. While rolls are rising to double, preheat oven to 400°F.

8. Place in oven, immediately lowering temperature to 350°F, and bake for 20 minutes, until golden brown.

Notes...

Video: Sweet Potato Orange Rolls

Gluten-Free Dinner Rolls

Ingredients

5 eggs
1 1/2 cups warm buttermilk
1/4 cup organic agave
1/4 cup extra virgin olive oil
4 teaspoons xanthan gum
1/2 cup flax seeds, soaked in 1 cup water for at least 1 hour
1/2 cup potato starch
1 tablespoon salt
1/2 cup buckwheat flour, freshly ground
5 cups gluten-free flour, freshly ground (reserve 1/2 cup flour for making rolls)
1/4 cup instant yeast

Yield: 2 dozen

Directions

1. In WonderMix bowl, with dough hook, place ingredients.
2. Mix well for 2 minutes. This dough should be more like heavy cake batter rather than bread dough.
3. To make rolls, scoop batter into flour and roll.
4. Place in cake pan, leaving space between.
5. Let rise to double.
6. While rolls are rising, preheat oven to 400°F.
7. Place in oven, immediately lowering temperature to 350°F, and bake for 20 minutes, until golden brown.

These are amazing rolls — light and tasty.

Use a freshly-ground blend of three or more gluten-free grains.

Notes . . .

Video: Gluten-Free All-Purpose Dough

Burger Buns

To make these buns, I mostly use a good white flour and add other whole grains to add nutrition and variety. My personal favorite flour options are red quinoa flour, buckwheat flour, whole popped amaranth, red rice flour, and black rice flour.

Ingredients

- 4 eggs
- 4 cups warm water
- 1/2 cup cooking oil
- 4 tablespoons organic agave
- 2/3 cup nonfat dry milk
- 2 teaspoons salt
- 2 cups whole-grain flour, your choice
- 10 cups Natural White flour
- 4 tablespoons instant yeast
- Toppings: Egg white and sesame seeds

Yield: 2 dozen

Directions

1. In WonderMix bowl, with dough hook, place ingredients, with yeast on top.
2. Turn on mixer. Make sure to add white flour only until dough pulls away from sides of bowl.
3. Mix for 6 minutes.
4. Remove and divide into 24 pieces.
5. For burger buns: Roll into balls, using your cupped hand. Flatten into burger-size circles. Place on parchment paper, 6 to a pan, leaving plenty of room for them to grow.
6. For hot dog buns: Roll pieces to about 5 inches long. Flatten and fold dough to the center, pinching to keep together. Place seam down on parchment paper.
7. Brush with egg white and sprinkle with sesame seeds.
8. Let rise to double.
9. While buns are rising, preheat oven to 400°F.
10. Bake for 5 minutes and then reduce temperature to 325°F and bake for another 6 to 10 minutes.

Variation:

Bacon Burger Buns: Add 1 cup cooked chopped bacon pieces to the dough. Use the bacon drippings for the oil.

Kalamata Olive and Feta Burger Buns: Add chopped olives to the dough. The last minute of kneading, add 1 cup (or more) feta cheese.

Golden Raisin Blue Cheese Burger Buns: Add 1 cup golden raisins to the dough. The last 30 seconds of kneading, add 1 cup crumbled firm blue cheese.

Once you get the hang of making your own burger buns, you will never want to use store-bought buns again.

Video: Black Peppercorn Rosemary Potato Rolls

Gluten-Free Burger Buns

Ingredients

5 eggs
2 cups warm milk
1/4 cup extra virgin olive oil
1/3 cup organic agave
1/2 cup potato starch
1 tablespoon salt
4 teaspoons xanthan gum
1/2 cup flax meal
4 cups gluten-free flour, freshly ground on pastry setting
5 tablespoons instant yeast
Toppings: Egg wash and sesame seeds

Yield: 2 dozen

Directions

1. In WonderMix bowl, with dough hook and dough divider insert, place ingredients, with yeast on top.

2. Mix well for 5 minutes. This dough should be more like heavy cake batter rather than bread dough.

3. With a large ice cream scoop, scoop out dough on to parchment paper, sprinkled with gluten-free flour. For slider-size buns, use a smaller scoop.

4. With a moist hand, pat down dough to a circle, about an inch thick.

5. Let rise to double.

6. While buns are rising, preheat oven to 400°F.

7. Brush with an egg wash and sprinkle with sesame seeds.

8. Put in oven and immediately reduce heat to 350°F and bake for 12 to 17 minutes, or until golden brown.

I love these buns. I think they're actually better than regular burger buns. I like changing out the grains. Red rice gives them color and texture.

When grinding gluten-free grains, keep in mind that a blend of three or more grains works well (such as a combination of red rice, quinoa, amaranth, sorghum, teff, or buckwheat. That's the secret of WonderFlour™!

Notes . . .

Video: Gluten-Free All-Purpose Dough

Banana Bread Plus

This makes a wonderfully healthful banana bread — great for snacks. Any whole-grain flour works well in this banana bread.

To make sour milk for baking, put 1 tablespoon vinegar or lemon juice per cup of milk. Let it stand for 5 minutes before using.

Ingredients

- 4 ripe bananas, mashed
- 2 small red potatoes, cooked tender
- 1 stick butter, or 1/2 cup unmelted coconut oil
- 1 1/4 cups sour milk, or buttermilk
- 2 teaspoons baking soda, added to the sour milk
- 2 teaspoons vanilla
- 1 teaspoon salt
- 2 cups coconut sugar, or 1 1/2 cups organic agave
- 4 cups WonderFlour™, freshly ground and sifted, or Gluten-Free WonderFlour™
- 1 cup nuts, chopped

Yield: 4 small loaves

Directions

1. Preheat oven to 350°F.
2. In WonderMix bowl, with French whips, place bananas and cooked potatoes.
3. Mash together.
4. Add butter (or coconut oil), sour milk (with soda), vanilla, salt, and sugar.
5. Add sifted flour and nuts.
6. Mix well.
7. Place in pans sprayed with non-stick pan spray.
8. Bake for about 1 hour, depending on pan.

To test for doneness: Place a toothpick in the center of the bread. When it comes out dry, the banana bread is done.

GF To make this recipe gluten free, just use a blend of gluten-free grains, freshly ground in your WonderMill. I have found that for most recipes that do not use yeast, you can use a blend of gluten-free grains and it works well. Amaranth, brown rice, sorghum, quinoa, teff, and buckwheat are all great grains to use.

Notes ...

Old-Fashioned Cornbread

Ingredients

2 eggs
2 1/3 cups milk
1/2 cup canola oil
3/4 cup sugar, or 1/2 cup organic agave
2 cups popcorn, freshly ground
2 cups WonderFlour™, or 2 cups amaranth flour, freshly ground
1 teaspoon salt
2 tablespoons baking powder
2 tablespoons bacon drippings, or butter (for pan)

Yield: 1 pan

Directions

1 Preheat oven to 400°F.

2 In WonderMix bowl, with French whips, mix all ingredients for 2 minutes.

3 In oven, place cast iron skillet with 2 tablespoons bacon drippings (or butter, but bacon fat is better!).

4 When skillet is very hot, pour in batter.

5 Place back in oven and bake for about 35 or 40 minutes, or until a toothpick comes out clean.

Notes . . .

I grind popcorn in my WonderMill on the coarsest setting. It grinds perfectly. For any recipe that calls for cornmeal, I substitute with popcorn, ground in my WonderMill.

Cornbread is easy to make gluten-free. Just use gluten-free flour. It actually changes the flavor of cornbread for the better.

I love the depth of taste that grains add to foods. Using freshly-ground popcorn is actually the most amazing part of baking cornbread. Popcorn has less starch and makes a better cornbread that does not crumble.

Cinnamon Rolls

There should never be anything healthy about a cinnamon roll!

Ingredients

- 3 eggs
- 3 cups warm buttermilk
- 1 cups sourdough starter
- 1/2 cup sugar
- 1/2 stick butter, melted
- 1 tablespoon salt
- 5 to 8 cups (to begin with) high-gluten white flour
- 2 1/2 tablespoons instant yeast
- Toppings: Melted butter and cinnamon/brown sugar mixture

Yield: 2 dozen

Maple Frosting

- 1/2 stick butter, melted
- 1 8-oz. pkg. cream cheese, room temperature
- 1 tablespoon maple extract
- Enough heavy cream to smooth frosting
- 8 cups powdered sugar

Whisk together in food processor until smooth.

Directions

1. In WonderMix bowl, with dough hook, place ingredients, with yeast on top.
2. With mixer turned on, add enough flour for dough to clean sides of bowl.
3. Mix for 6 minutes. Remove from bowl and place in large, oiled bowl.
4. Let rise until double. (Remember, a sticky dough makes the best rolls.)
5. Remove from bowl and divide dough into 4 equal pieces. Placing one piece on rolling surface, roll dough out into large semi-circle.
6. Top with melted butter and then a cinnamon and brown sugar mixture.
7. Sprinkle lightly with water and roll up dough, starting from furthest away. Roll towards you, pulling dough tight.
8. Cut in half, then cut halves in half. Cut each piece then into 3 pieces. You should end up with 12 rolls.
9. Place rolls into pan, sprayed with non-stick pan spray, leaving a small space in between each roll.
10. Let rise until double in size.
11. While cinnamon rolls are rising, preheat oven to 400°F.
12. Bake for 5 minutes, then reduce temperature to 325°F for an additional 12 to 15 minutes. Do not over-bake; this dries out the cinnamon rolls.

Video: Sourdough Starter

Gluten-Free Cinnamon Rolls

Ingredients

5 eggs
2 cups warm milk
1/3 cup organic agave
1/4 cup coconut oil
4 teaspoons xanthan gum
2 teaspoons salt
1/2 cup potato starch
4 1/2 cups gluten-free flour, freshly ground
1/4 cup instant yeast
Toppings: Melted butter and cinnamon/sugar mixture; butter

Yield: 2 dozen

Directions

1. In WonderMix bowl, with dough hook, place ingredients, with yeast on top.
2. Mix well for 5 minutes. This dough should be more like heavy cake batter rather than bread dough.
3. Divide dough into 2 pieces. Place on gluten-free floured surface. Place half the dough on surface and sprinkle with gluten-free flour.
4. Roll dough to a 1/4-inch thickness.
5. Drizzle with melted butter and cover with cinnamon and sugar mixture.
6. Roll dough up and cut like rolls. Place rolls in pan, sprayed with non-stick pan spray, and top each roll with a dab of butter.
7. Let rise. It will take them longer to rise than regular cinnamon rolls.
8. While cinnamon rolls are rising, preheat oven to 400°F.
9. Put in oven, immediately reducing temperature to 350°F, and bake for 20 minutes, or until golden brown.

You're never going to get a real cinnamon roll without the gluten but this is a close second. I like these cinnamon rolls warm, topped with a maple frosting.

Cinnamon/Sugar Mixture
3 cups sugar, or coconut sugar
1/4 cup cinnamon

Cinnamon rolls are really hard to do gluten free. This recipe is great, however. Make sure to let the cinnamon rolls rise — it will take a while.

Video: Gluten-Free All-Purpose Dough

Breads

Zucchini Loaves

I love a good zucchini loaf and just changing the grain can make a huge difference to the taste and texture. Experiment until you find the perfect combination for you.

Ingredients

3 eggs, lightly beaten
1 cup buttermilk
3/4 cup vegetable oil, or coconut oil
2 teaspoons vanilla
1 1/2 cups sugar, or coconut sugar or 1 cup organic agave
2 cups zucchini, shredded
4 cups spelt flour, freshly ground, or WonderFlour™
1/2 cup flax meal
1 teaspoon salt
1 teaspoon baking soda
2 teaspoons baking powder
3 teaspoons baking spice

Yield: 4 small loaves

Directions

1 Preheat oven to 350°F.

2 In WonderMix bowl, with French whips, combine all ingredients and mix well.

3 Spoon into loaf pans and bake for 45 minutes.

4 Cool and cover with Glaze and chopped pecans.

GF

We miss this type of bread when we go gluten free. No reason to do that. Gluten free is easy and fun. To make this recipe gluten-free, simply change out the flours to a gluten-free blend. Remember that a blend of three or more grains ups the success rate to 100%.

Coconut sugar and organic agave nectar are both low on the glycemic index — great for diabetics and great if you are watching your sugar intake.

Glaze

1 cup powdered sugar
1 teaspoon vanilla
2 to 3 tablespoons coconut oil
2 teaspoons lemon extract
Topping: Pecans, chopped

Mix together and drizzle over loaves. Top with chopped pecans.

These Zucchini Loaves are so healthful. Whole grain, good oil, and a great sweetener make them perfect.

Bread Pudding

Nothing like a bread pudding — and it's a great way to use up old bread or too much bread when you're baking.

This recipe is easy to make gluten free. Just use gluten-free breads! **GF**

Ingredients

- 4 large eggs
- 1 cup sugar
- 1 tablespoon vanilla
- 2 cups half and half
- 1 teaspoon nutmeg
- 2 teaspoons cinnamon
- 4 tablespoons butter, melted, plus 2 more for top
- 12 slices bread, or 8 cups assorted breads, cut up
- 2 cups fresh fruit (optional)

Yield: 1 large pan

Directions

1. Preheat oven to 350°F.
2. In bowl, whisk together eggs, sugar, vanilla, half and half, nutmeg, cinnamon, and melted butter.
3. In another large bowl, place bread and top with mixture. It should be moist.
4. Add fruit, if desired.
5. Place in oven-proof dish that has been sprayed with non-stick pan spray.
6. Top with butter.
7. Bake for 40 minutes. Make sure it is done but don't over-bake.
8. Remove from oven and add Glaze.

Glaze

- 2 tablespoons butter
- 1/4 cup half and half
- Powdered sugar
- Vanilla, or maple extract

(If I add fruit, I use vanilla; if I do just bread, I do a maple glaze.)

Whole-Grain Croutons

Ingredients

10 cups of cubed bread, whole-grain or gluten-free bread
3/4 cup (or more) olive oil, or butter
2 tablespoons Italian-style seasonings
1 cup Parmesan cheese, finely grated
1 tablespoon salt
2 tablespoons pepper, freshly ground

Yield: Never enough

Directions

1. Preheat oven to 350°F.
2. In large bowl, place cubed bread.
3. In separate bowl, whisk other ingredients and drizzle over cubed bread.
4. Toss well.
5. Place on jelly roll pans, lined with parchment paper, and bake to golden brown, stirring occasionally to ensure even toasting.
6. Remove from oven and cool.
7. Store in airtight container until needed.

Croutons are a great way to get rid of excess bread. The up side is they are fresh and whole grain, packed with flavor. I like to snack on them.

Make gluten-free croutons by using cubed gluten-free breads. **GF**

Croutons can be totally changed by using different herbs and spices. Be creative and have fun creating your own style to fit your needs and taste.

Baking is not, or should not be, a stressful process. If you are stressed, you are doing something wrong. Take a deep breath — maybe a few — and relax and enjoy the experience.

Notes . . .

Gluten-Free Almond Butter Cake

This recipe works well with any blend of grains. A great combination for this recipe is oat groats, amaranth, and sorghum.

Using freshly ground gluten-free grains will make this scrumptious cake even better.

Ingredients

- 2 sticks butter
- 1 cup organic agave
- 3 eggs
- 1 teaspoon almond extract
- 2 cups gluten-free grains, freshly ground on pastry setting and sifted
- 1/4 cup almond flour
- 3 tablespoons potato starch
- 2 teaspoons baking powder
- 1/4 teaspoon salt
- 1 cup milk

Directions

1. Preheat oven to 350°F.
2. In WonderMix bowl, with French whips, cream butter and agave until creamy.
3. Add eggs and almond extract, and cream together.
4. In separate bowl, sift together flours, potato starch, baking powder, and salt.
5. Add milk and dry ingredients in stages of three. Don't over-beat.
6. Place in two 9-inch cake pans, sprayed with non-stick pan spray.
7. Bake until a toothpick comes out clean, about 20 minutes.
8. Frost when cool.

Frosting

- 1 8-oz. pkg. cream cheese
- 1/4 cup milk
- 1 cup almonds, slivered
- 1/2 stick butter, melted
- 1 teaspoon almond extract
- Powdered sugar
- Topping: Almonds

1. In WonderMix bowl, with French whips, add cream cheese, melted butter, and almond extract.
2. Blend well. Add powdered sugar until smooth and thick.
3. Frost cake and top with almonds.

Sifting flours lifts and aerates them, removing heavier parts of the grain. This is especially helpful when using whole grains for baking. It makes your baked goods lighter. Reserve the bran and heavier parts for muffins, or even hot cereal for breakfast.

Cakes

Fresh Apple Cake

This cake is great. The caramel sauce is a bit spicy but oh how wonderful the spicy and sweet combo.

GF Use freshly ground Gluten-Free Wonder-Flour™ to make this gluten free.

Notes . . .

Ingredients

- 3 to 4 large baking apples
- 1 cup coconut oil
- 1 1/2 cups organic agave, or coconut sugar
- 4 eggs
- 1 cup buttermilk
- 2 teaspoons vanilla
- 3 cups spelt flour, freshly ground, or gluten-free flour blend
- 1 tablespoon baking powder
- 1 tablespoon pumpkin pie spice
- 2 tablespoons chipotle chili, pureed
- 1 teaspoon salt
- 1 cup pistachio nuts, chopped

Directions

1. Preheat oven to 350°F.
2. Grate apples with mandolin on the fine grate.
3. In WonderMix bowl, with French whips, place oil, agave (or sugar), eggs, buttermilk, and vanilla. Whip until a mayonnaise-like texture.
4. Add remaining ingredients and place in a large pan.
5. Bake 35 to 45 minutes.
6. Serve topped with Chipotle Caramel Sauce.

Chipotle Caramel Sauce
(Optional)
- 2 sticks butter
- 1 cup brown sugar
- 1 cup heavy cream
- 2 tablespoons chipotle chili, pureed, or 2 teaspoons chipotle powder

Topping: Whipped cream

1. Bring butter and sugar to boil.
2. Add cream and chili and simmer.
3. Serve over hot cake with dollop of whipped cream.

Spelt Pickled Lemon Bread

One of my favorite breads.

To make gluten free, simply change out the spelt flour with gluten-free flour. GF

Ingredients

- 3 1/2 cups spelt flour, freshly ground, or WonderFlour™ or Gluten-Free WonderFlour™
- 1 tablespoon baking powder
- 1 teaspoon salt
- 2 cups organic sugar, or 1 1/2 cups organic agave
- 4 large eggs
- 1 12-oz. can evaporated milk (reserve 1/4 cup for Glaze)
- 2/3 cup vegetable oil, or coconut oil
- 4 sections pickled lemons, or 1/2 cup lemon juice and zest from 2 lemons
- 2 teaspoons vanilla

Directions

1. Preheat oven to 350°F.
2. In large bowl, place dry ingredients and mix well.
3. In WonderMix blender, place eggs, milk, oil, vanilla, and lemons.
4. Blend well.
5. In WonderMix bowl, with French whips, combine dry ingredients with blended ingredients and mix well.
6. Place in 2 large loaf pans, sprayed with non-stick pan spray.
7. Bake for 45 to 50 minutes.
8. Remove from oven and place on rack.
9. Let cool before adding Glaze.

Glaze

- 1 pickled lemon
- 1/4 cup evaporated canned milk
- 2 teaspoons vanilla
- 2 tablespoons coconut oil
- 3 generous cups of powdered sugar

1. In WonderMix blender, place lemon, milk, vanilla, and coconut oil.
2. Mix until lemon is smooth. Add sugar and blend until glaze is smooth.
3. Place breads on a rack and glaze.

Cakes made with whole grains are going to be different than those made with white flour. Yes, they will be heavier but don't let that stop you. Try different grains until you find the combination you like. I love the texture of whole grains in my cakes. When I use them, I don't feel quite so guilty when I eat a few slices.

Cakes

Short Cake

Ingredients

- 6 1/2 cups spelt flour, freshly ground on pastry setting and sifted, or WonderFlour™ or Gluten-Free WonderFlour™
- 6 tablespoons baking powder
- 1/3 cup sugar
- 1 tablespoon salt
- 2 sticks butter, cut into 1/2-inch pieces
- About 2 cups heavy cream
- Topping: Raw sugar

Directions

1. Preheat oven to 400°F.
2. In WonderMix bowl, with French whips, place flour with baking powder, sugar, and salt. Whip.
3. Add butter and cut in with whips.
4. Replace whips with dough hook.
5. Turn on mixer and drizzle cream over mixture until a dough forms.
6. Knead for 1 minute.
7. Remove and place on floured counter.
8. Roll out. Cut with biscuit cutter.
9. Place on parchment paper and sprinkle with raw sugar.
10. Bake for about 12 minutes, or until golden brown.

This is a family favorite. Gluten-free or not, we love the tender, light texture and how great it tastes with strawberries and cream.

GF To make gluten free, just replace the spelt with a gluten-free flour, like Gluten-Free WonderFlour™.

Our families love treats. Make them as healthful as you can without compromising flavor or texture. With whole grains, it is possible and enjoyable!

Notes . . .

Spelt Chocolate Cupcakes

This recipe is a wonderful recipe that dates back 40 years or more. It was found in a collection of recipes of a man, now deceased, who had worked in a bakery in his youth. This recipe had "good" written across the bottom of the page. It really is good — and it can double as a chocolate cake.

GF *Replace the spelt flour with Gluten-Free WonderFlour™ to make this recipe gluten free.*

Ingredients

- 1/2 cup spelt flour, freshly ground, or WonderFlour™ or Gluten-Free Wonder-Flour™
- 1/2 cup powdered sugar
- 1 1/2 cups organic agave
- 1 teaspoon salt
- 2 teaspoons baking soda
- 2 teaspoons vanilla
- Pinch of cinnamon
- 6 eggs
- 1 cup buttermilk
- 1 1/2 cups spelt flour, freshly ground, or WonderFlour™ or Gluten-Free WonderFlour™
- 1/2 cup powdered sugar
- 1/2 cup baking cocoa powder
- 1 teaspoon baking powder

Yield: 2 dozen

Directions

1. Preheat oven to 350°F.
2. In WonderMix bowl, with French whips, cream together first 7 ingredients.
3. Add eggs, one at a time.
4. Whisk in buttermilk.
5. In separate bowl, whisk together flour, powdered sugar, cocoa powder, and baking powder.
6. Add dry ingredients to creamed mixture.
7. Beat until smooth.
8. Fill cupcake liners 3/4 full.
9. Bake for about 16 minutes.
10. Top with Chocolate Butter Cream Frosting.
11. This recipe can also be used for layer cakes or sheet cakes.

Chocolate Butter Cream Frosting

- 2 sticks unsalted butter, softened
- 3 to 4 cups powdered sugar, sifted
- 1/4 teaspoon salt
- 1/4 cup baking cocoa powder
- 1 tablespoon vanilla
- Up to 4 tablespoons milk, or heavy cream

1. In WonderMix, with French whips, beat butter.
2. Add 3 cups powdered sugar. Beat. Add vanilla, salt, and 2 tablespoons milk (or cream). Beat for 3 minutes.
3. Add powdered sugar until right consistency. To thin, add remaining milk, 1 tablespoon at a time.

Cakes

Carrot Cake

You will never know there's a whole grain in this delightfully moist carrot cake.

To make gluten free, use Gluten-Free WonderFlour™ instead of spelt. (GF)

Coconut oils are a great substitute for butter and oils in recipes. Extra virgin coconut oil has the wonderful coconut flavor. Refined has had the coconut flavor removed — ideal for those who do not like the flavor or for recipes where you don't want a coconut flavor.

Ingredients

- 3 eggs
- 3 cups coconut sugar, or 2 1/2 cups organic agave
- 1 cup coconut oil
- 1 stick butter
- 3 cups spelt flour, freshly ground and sifted, or WonderFlour™ or Gluten-Free WonderFlour™
- 2 teaspoons salt
- 1 tablespoon baking soda
- 6 teaspoons cinnamon
- 1 teaspoon nutmeg
- 1/2 teaspoon cloves
- 2 tablespoons vanilla
- 1 1/4 cups crushed pineapple
- 2 apples, grated
- 1 cup coconut
- 1 1/3 cups carrots, cooked and pureed
- 1 1/2 cups walnuts

Directions

1. Preheat oven to 350°F.
2. In WonderMix bowl, with French whips, mix together eggs, sugar (or agave), coconut oil, and butter until light.
3. Add rest of ingredients and mix well.
4. Place in large, well-greased cake pan.
5. Bake for about 35 minutes.
6. Remove from oven, cool, and frost.

Cream Cheese Frosting

- 1 8-oz. pkg. cream cheese, softened
- 6 tablespoons butter, softened
- 3 1/2 cups powdered sugar
- 1 teaspoon vanilla
- Zest and juice of one lemon
- 1/4 teaspoon lemon extract

1. Combine softened cream cheese and butter and mix well.
2. Add rest of the ingredients and mix until light and easy to spread.

Whole-Grain Walnut Bundt Cake

Ingredients

For the Streusel:
- 1/2 cup brown sugar
- 1 cup spelt flour, freshly ground, or WonderFlour™ or Gluten-Free WonderFlour™
- 2 teaspoons baking spice, or cinnamon
- Dash salt
- 6 tablespoons butter, cut into pieces
- 1 cup nuts

For the Cake:
- 1 1/2 sticks butter, room temperature
- 1 3/4 cups coconut sugar
- 3 large eggs
- 2 teaspoons vanilla
- 1 1/2 cups sour cream
- 3 cups spelt flour, freshly ground
- 2 teaspoons baking soda
- 1 teaspoon baking powder
- 1/2 teaspoon kosher salt

Directions

For the Streusel:
1. In WonderMix bowl, with French whips, place all ingredients.
2. Turn on mixer and mix until ingredients are coarsely mixed.
3. Remove from mixer bowl and place in small bowl. Set aside.

For the Cake:
1. Preheat oven to 350°F.
2. In WonderMix bowl, with French whips, place butter and sugar. Mix well.
3. Add eggs, one at a time, and mix.
4. Add vanilla and sour cream. Mix. Add remaining ingredients and mix well.
5. Place half the batter in bundt cake pan.
6. Place 3/4 of the streusel over batter.
7. Pour remaining batter evenly over streusel.
8. Place remaining streusel over batter.
9. Bake until done, about 45 to 50 minutes. Test with a toothpick. Toothpick will come out clean when done.

This cake is so moist and tender, you'll never believe it's whole grain.

GF — To make this recipe gluten free, use Gluten-Free WonderFlour™ instead of the spelt or regular WonderFlour™.

Glaze
- 2 tablespoons coconut oil
- 1/4 cup heavy cream, or buttermilk
- 2 teaspoons vanilla
- 3 cups powdered sugar
- 1/2 cup nuts, chopped, for garnish

1. In WonderMix blender, place melted coconut oil, cream (or buttermilk), and vanilla.
2. Add powdered sugar and blend.
3. Pour over cooled cake.
4. Top with chopped walnuts, if desired.
5. Keep covered and enjoy. It will actually taste better the next day.

Yellow Lemon Cake

If you want to make a white cake, add vanilla and extra milk in place of the lemon juice and zest.

Use Gluten-Free WonderFlour™ to make this recipe gluten free.

Having a good quality grain mill is essential to producing healthful, whole-grain baked goods. Flours, ground fresh, retain all the nutrients and are optimal for performance and taste.

Ingredients

- 2 1/2 cups Wonder-Flour™, freshly ground and sifted, or Gluten-Free WonderFlour™ or spelt flour
- 2 teaspoons baking powder
- 1/2 teaspoon salt
- 5 large egg yolks (whites reserved)
- 1/2 cup coconut oil
- 1 cup organic agave
- 1/3 cup buttermilk
- 1/3 cup lemon juice
- 1 tablespoon lemon zest, freshly grated
- 5 large egg whites
- 1/4 teaspoon cream of tartar

Directions

1. Preheat oven to 350°F.
2. Lightly grease two 9" round cake pans, lined with lightly greased parchment paper. Set aside.
3. In medium bowl, whisk together sifted flour, baking powder, and salt. Set aside.
4. Using a stand mixer or hand mixer, combine egg yolks and oil. Beat at low speed.
5. As mixture thickens, slowly add agave.
6. Add buttermilk and lemon juice. Beat on medium speed for 3 minutes, stopping occasionally to scrape bottom and sides of bowl.
7. Gently fold in flour mixture and lemon zest with rubber spatula.
8. In separate bowl, free of any oil or grease, beat egg whites until foamy.
9. Add cream of tartar and continue to beat on high speed until soft peaks form.
10. Gently fold beaten whites into batter by thirds. Combine only until traces of white remain. Don't over-mix.
11. Divide cake batter between 2 pans. Bake 20 to 25 minutes, until a cake tester tests clean and cake begins to pull away from sides of pan. For a 9" x 13" pan, bake 25 to 35 minutes. For cupcakes, bake 15 to 18 minutes.
12. Cool in pan for 10 minutes before turning out on to a rack to cool completely.
13. Frost, as desired.

Cookies & Crackers 63

Whole-Grain Chocolate Chip Cookies

Ingredients

2 sticks butter
1 cup sugar
1 cup brown sugar
2 eggs
1 tablespoon vanilla
1 teaspoon salt
1 teaspoon baking soda
3 to 3 1/2 cups spelt flour, freshly ground, or WonderFlour™ or Gluten-Free WonderFlour™
2 cups chocolate chips
1 cups nuts, chopped (optional)

Yield: 3 dozen

Directions

1. Preheat oven to 350°F.

2. In WonderMix bowl, with cookie whips, whip butter and sugar until creamy.

3. Add eggs and vanilla. Whip until creamy.

4. Replace whips with dough hook.

5. Add dry ingredients and mix well.

6. Scoop cookie dough on to cookie sheet, lined with parchment paper.

7. Bake until done, about 10 to 12 minutes.

Once you get used to whole-grain cookies, it's hard to eat cookies made with white flour.

GF To make this recipe gluten free, use Gluten-Free WonderFlour™.

Baking powder reacts to moisture and baking soda reacts to heat. When making cookies use baking soda.

Don't give up on the first attempt. Change the grains and change the experience. Different grains act and taste differently. Some you might not like. Don't stop there — try the recipe again with a different combination of grains.

Notes . . .

Whole-Grain Oatmeal Cookies

I love these wonderful whole-grain cookies. The coconut sugar gives them a dark appearance and a wonderfully rich flavor.

GF To make these cookies gluten free, use Gluten-Free WonderFlour™ — and be sure to use gluten-free oatmeal. Not all oatmeals are created equal.

Ingredients

- 4 sticks butter
- 4 cups coconut sugar
- 4 eggs
- 1 tablespoon vanilla
- 4 cups flour, freshly ground
- 6 cups oatmeal
- 2 teaspoons baking soda
- 2 teaspoons salt
- 1 tablespoon cinnamon
- 2 teaspoons nutmeg
- 2 cups golden raisins
- 2 cups nuts, chopped

Yield: 3 dozen

Directions

1. Preheat oven to 350°F.
2. In WonderMix, with cookie whips, cream together butter and sugar.
3. Add eggs and vanilla. Cream together.
4. In a separate bowl, sift all dry ingredients.
5. Replace whips with dough hook. Add dry ingredients and mix well.
6. Scoop unto cookie sheet, lined with parchment paper.
7. Bake until golden brown, 10 to 12 minutes.

Cookies & Crackers

Italian Cornmeal Cookies

Ingredients

- 1 stick butter, room temperature
- 1/2 cup sugar, or coconut sugar
- 3 large eggs
- 1 teaspoon orange extract, or 3 to 4 drops orange essential oil
- 1 1/4 cups Wonder-Flour™, freshly ground, or Gluten-Free WonderFlour™
- 1 1/4 cups cornmeal, freshly ground
- 6 tablespoons pine nuts, or chopped almonds
- 1 teaspoon fennel seeds, and/or 1/4 cup cocoa nibs
- 1 teaspoon baking soda
- 1/4 teaspoon salt
- 1 cup dark raisins, or Craisins

Yield: 3 dozen

Directions

1. Preheat oven to 375°F.
2. In WonderMix bowl, with cookie whips, cream together butter and sugar.
3. Add eggs and orange zest, and cream together until light and fluffy.
4. Replace whips with dough hook. Add flour, cornmeal, nuts, seeds, cocoa nibs, soda, salt, and raisins.
5. Mix well.
6. Scoop on to parchment paper.
7. Bake until golden brown around the edges, about 12 minutes.

This is really a wonderful dipping cookie. Don't expect a cookie texture, however. This cookie is really dense but I love the texture and the flavor. Perfect with a cup of cocoa.

GF Freshly ground Gluten-Free WonderFlour™ gives a boost in nutrition and flavor.

Cookies & Crackers

Basil Spice Cookies

This cookie resembles a gourmet ginger snap. I love these cookies. They are so full of flavor. The fresh basil and Garam Masala make them so unusual, you will love them.

Freshly ground Gluten-Free WonderFlour™ is a great way to make this recipe gluten free.

GF

Ingredients

- 2 sticks butter, softened
- 2 cups coconut sugar
- 2 eggs
- 1 tablespoon vanilla
- 1 cup basil, chopped (place eggs and basil in blender and pulse until chopped)
- 4 cups WonderFlour™, or Gluten-Free WonderFlour™
- 1 teaspoon salt
- 2 teaspoons Garam Masala spice
- 1 teaspoon baking soda
- Chocolate chips and nuts (optional)

Yield: 3 dozen

Garam Masala is a blend of aromatic Indian spices.

Directions

1. Preheat oven to 350°F.
2. In WonderMix bowl, with cookie whips, place soft butter and sugar.
3. Whip until creamy.
4. Add eggs, vanilla, and basil. Whip until well blended.
5. Replace whips with dough hook. Add dry ingredients. Mix well.
6. Add chips and/or nuts, if desired.
7. Bake for 10 to 13 minutes, or until light brown. Do not over-bake. Cookies are better slightly under-cooked and cooled to remain soft.
8. Dough can be made and kept in the refrigerator for quick cooking.

Cookies & Crackers 67

Red Quinoa Coconut Cookies

Ingredients

- 2 cups white sugar
- 2 cups brown sugar
- 4 sticks butter, room temperature
- 4 eggs
- 1 tablespoon vanilla
- 2 teaspoons salt
- 2 teaspoons baking soda
- 6 cups WonderFlour™, or Gluten-Free Wonder-Flour™
- 3 cups fine unsweetened coconut
- 2 cups red quinoa, cooked and chilled
- Good quality chocolate, for dipping

Yield: 3 dozen

Directions

1. Preheat oven to 350°F.
2. In WonderMix bowl, with cookie whips, place sugar and butter. Cream together.
3. Add eggs and vanilla. Cream together until well mixed.
4. Replace whips with dough hook. Add remaining ingredients and mix well.
5. Scoop on to cookie sheet, lined with parchment paper. Wet hands and flatten cookies before baking.
6. Bake for 10 to 12 minutes, until golden brown.
7. Remove from oven and let cool. They will stick to the parchment. After they are cooled, just flip over the parchment and peel it from the cookies.
8. After chilling, dip in melted chocolate.

These are my favorite cookies ever. Dipped in chocolate, they are so amazing. I love the red quinoa texture and flavor.

To make this recipe gluten free, use Gluten-Free WonderFlour™. **GF**

To Dip:

1. Melt dipping chocolate.
2. Dip cookies and place on parchment paper.
3. Place in refrigerator for a couple of minutes to harden.

Cookies & Crackers

Whole-Grain Pecan Bars

Ingredients

For the Crust:
- 1 stick butter
- 3/4 cup coconut sugar
- 1 cup whole-grain flour (spelt, brown rice, WonderFlour™, or Gluten-Free WonderFlour™)
- 1 teaspoon baking powder
- 1 teaspoon sea salt
- 1/2 cup pecans, chopped

For the Filling:
- 6 tablespoons butter, melted
- 1/2 cup coconut sugar
- 1/2 cup organic agave
- 2 teaspoons vanilla
- 1/2 teaspoon salt
- 1 egg and 1 egg yolk
- 2 cups pecans, chopped

Yield: 3 dozen

Directions

For the Crust:
1. Preheat oven to 350°F.
2. In food processor, place ingredients for crust. Mix well in food processor until it resembles peas.
3. Place in buttered 9"-square baking pan. Pat down well.
4. Bake for 15 to 20 minutes.
5. While baking, prepare filling.

For the Filling:
1. In a bowl, mix all ingredients for the filling.
2. Place on top of cooked crust.
3. Bake for 25 minutes.
4. Let cool, then cut into squares.

Unexpectedly delightful!

GF — Use a blend of gluten-free whole grains to make these delectable pecan bars gluten free.

If cookies are coming out dry, cut back on the flour.

Notes . . .

Bacon Toffee Cookies

Bacon is great in anything. The combination of sweet and salty is so satisfying to our taste buds. This cookie is perfect.

GF To make gluten free, simply use gluten-free flour, such as Gluten-Free WonderFlour™.

Ingredients

- 2 sticks butter
- 1 cup sugar
- 1 cup brown sugar
- 2 eggs
- 1 tablespoon vanilla
- 1 teaspoon salt
- 1 teaspoon baking powder
- 3 1/2 cups spelt, freshly ground, WonderFlour™ or Gluten-Free Wonder-Flour™ (but any flour will do)
- 1 heaping cup crispy fried bacon
- 2 cups toffee pieces
- 1 cup chocolate chips

Yield: 3 dozen

Directions

1. Preheat oven to 350°F.
2. In WonderMix, with cookie whips, whip butter and sugar together until creamy.
3. Add eggs and vanilla. Whip until creamy.
4. In separate bowl, combine dry ingredients.
5. Replace whips with dough hook. Add dry ingredients to creamed ingredients and mix well.
6. Add bacon, toffee, and chocolate chips. Mix until combined.
7. Scoop on to cookie sheet, lined with parchment paper. Gently press each cookie.
8. Bake until done, about 10 minutes, depending on size of cookie.

Video: Bacon Toffee Cookies

Cookies & Crackers

Spelt Buttermilk Cookies

Ingredients

- 1 1/2 sticks butter, or 3/4 cup unrefined coconut oil
- 1 1/2 cups organic agave
- 2 large eggs
- 1 teaspoon vanilla
- 3 1/2 cups spelt flour, freshly ground, or Gluten-Free WonderFlour™
- 1/2 teaspoon baking soda
- 1/2 teaspoon salt
- 1 teaspoon fresh lemon zest
- 1 cup coconut, shredded
- 1 cup pistachios, shelled, chopped and roaste

Yield: 3 dozen

Directions

1. Preheat oven to 350°F.
2. In WonderMix bowl, with cookie whips, beat butter and agave until fluffy.
3. Add eggs, one at a time, and vanilla.
4. Replace whips with dough hook. Add dry ingredients, zest, coconut, and nuts.
5. Mix, drizzling buttermilk over mixture.
6. When mixed, spoon tablespoon-size portions on to cookie sheet, lined with parchment paper.
7. Bake for 12 to 15 minutes, or until golden brown.
8. Remove from oven and cool. Top with Glaze.

This is a cake-style cookie, tender and light. Be sure to frost them.

Make this **GF** recipe gluten free by replacing the spelt flour with Gluten-Free WonderFlour™.

Glaze

- 1 1/2 cups powdered sugar
- Juice from one lemon (the one zested for the cookies works great)
- 3 tablespoons buttermilk
- Tiny pinch salt

Whisk together and lightly cover cookies with a thin coat of glaze.

Cookies & Crackers 73

Amaranth Cookies

Ingredients

- 2 cups coconut sugar
- 2 sticks butter, or 1 cup unmelted coconut oil
- 2 eggs
- 1 tablespoon vanilla
- 2 cups WonderFlour™ or Gluten-Free Wonder-Flour™
- 1 teaspoon baking soda
- 1 teaspoon baking powder
- 1 teaspoon salt
- 3 cups amaranth, popped
- 1 cup dried cranberries
- 1 1/2 cups chocolate chips (optional)

Yield: 3 dozen

Directions

1. Preheat oven to 350°F.
2. In WonderMix bowl, with cookie whips, place sugar, butter (or oil), eggs, and vanilla.
3. Cream together well.
4. Replace whips with dough hook. Add dry ingredients.
5. Mix well, adding popped amaranth, dried cranberries, and chocolate chips, if desired.
6. Drop cookies 2 inches apart on cookie sheet, lined with parchment paper.
7. Bake until light brown.

This is a classic oatmeal cookie — with an amaranth twist. Simply replace the oatmeal with popped amaranth and you have an amazing cookie!

To make gluten-free, use Gluten-Free WonderFlour™. (GF)

Popping Amaranth

1. Place deep saucepan over high heat.
2. Let pan heat up. When nice and hot, place pinch of amaranth in pan. It should pop quickly.
3. Once amaranth is popped, empty pan and add 1 or 2 tablespoons of whole-grain amaranth to pan.
4. Lift pan and gently shake, moving amaranth around. It will pop quickly.
5. Empty and place pan back on heat. Add more amaranth and start process again until you have desired amount.

To Store:

Popped amaranth stores well in an airtight container. I usually pop a lot at a time so I have it when I need it. Popped amaranth is great in and on so many things — from muffins to rice crispy treats.

Using different sugars changes the color and taste of cookies. We have been taught that white sugar is all we can use in cookies. That's just like saying white flour is all we can use. Totally false. There are so many more options.

Cookies & Crackers

Peanut Butter Cookies

Don't be alarmed by the dark color of the coconut sugar. These cookies are delicious.

If you use whole-grain oat flour, using gluten-free oats. Another option is to use Gluten-Free WonderFlour™. **GF**

Ingredients

- 2 sticks butter, softened
- 1 1/2 cups organic agave, or 2 cups coconut sugar
- 1 cup peanut butter
- 2 eggs
- 1 tablespoon vanilla
- 3 cups spelt flour, freshly ground, or whole-grain oat flour, or WonderFlour™ or Gluten-Free Wonder-Flour™
- 1 teaspoon salt
- 1 teaspoon baking soda
- 2 cups miniature peanut butter cups, chopped

Yield: 3 dozen

Directions

1. Preheat oven to 350°F.
2. In WonderMix bowl, with cookie whips, whip together butter, agave, and peanut butter.
3. Add eggs and vanilla. Whip until creamy.
4. Replace whips with dough hook.
5. Add dry ingredients.
6. Mix well, adding most of the chopped candy.
7. Scoop on to baking sheet, lined with parchment paper.
8. Press down with a fork.
9. Bake for 12 minutes.
10. These cookies are even better when frosted with a butter cream frosting — chocolate, of course.

Notes . . .

Parchment paper allows you to slide the entire pan of cookies off the cookie sheet on to the counter to cool quickly. This allows you to fill the pan again to bake the next batch.

Cookies & Crackers

Whole-Grain Toffee Cookies

I always bake one cookie first to see if I need more flour, or if I used too much. Baking one cookie can save a whole batch. If the cookie is flat like a pancake, just add more flour. If the cookie is hard like a hockey puck, simply moisten your hand and press the cookie flat on the tray. Bake as usual.

Ingredients

- 1 cup butter, or coconut oil
- 2 cups coconut sugar, or organic brown sugar
- 2 eggs
- 1 tablespoon vanilla
- 3 1/2 cups Wonder-Flour™, freshly ground, or spelt flour or Gluten-Free WonderFlour™
- 1 teaspoon salt
- 1 teaspoon baking soda
- 2 cups toffee pieces
- 1 cup nuts, chopped, (optional)
- 1 cup chocolate chips (optional)

Yield: 3 dozen

Directions

1. Preheat oven to 350°F.
2. In WonderMix bowl, with cookie whips, whip together sugar and butter (or coconut oil).
3. Add eggs and vanilla, and whip.
4. Sift flour with salt and baking soda, and mix. (If doubling the recipe, replace whips with dough hook.)
5. Add toffee pieces and desired optional ingredients. Mix well. Cookie batter should pull away from sides of bowl.
6. Scoop on to cookie sheet, lined with parchment paper.
7. Bake for 10 to 12 minutes.

GF Use gluten-free flour. Gluten-free flour changes the cookie, but I think it makes it better.

The best way to freeze baked goods to ensure quality is to freeze them as soon as they are cooled. If you place them in the freezer fresh, they usually come out fresh. If you wait until they're almost stale and old, freezing them will not bring them back. So freeze right away, especially for recipes that might be too large for you. The advantage is fresh-baked goods at a moment's notice.

Notes . . .

Cookies & Crackers 79

Basil Brownies

Ingredients

- 8 oz. unsweetened chocolate
- 2 1/2 sticks unsalted butter
- 6 large eggs
- 4 teaspoons vanilla
- 1 cup basil, chopped
- 3 1/2 cups granulated sugar
- 1 teaspoon salt
- 1 teaspoon orange oil extract, or 3 drops of orange essential oil
- 3 cups WonderFlour™, or spelt flour, freshly ground on pastry setting
- 2 cups walnuts, in pieces (optional)

Yield: 1 pan

Directions

1. Preheat oven to 350°F.
2. Line bar pan with foil or parchment paper, or grease pan with butter.
3. Melt chocolate and butter in a microwave oven, or in a saucepan over very low heat.
4. In WonderMix blender, place eggs, vanilla, and basil. Mix until basil is chopped well.
5. In WonderMix bowl, with cookie whips, place butter and sugar, and whip.
6. Add eggs and basil mixture. Cream again.
7. Add melted chocolate mixture and whisk to combine (mixture will thicken considerably).
8. Add all other ingredients and mix together until well combined.
9. Scrape batter into baking pan and bake about 50 minutes, or until cake tester comes out clean when inserted into center. For chewier brownies, bake an additional 5 to 10 minutes.
10. Let cool at least 2 hours in pan before icing (or sprinkling with sifted powdered sugar), removing, cutting, and serving.

I love these brownies. I love the basil and touch of orange. It's been a family favorite for years.

To make these brownies gluten-free, just replace the flour with your choice of gluten-free flour. **GF**

I always chop the basil with the nuts and then add them to the other ingredients.

Chocolate Cream Cheese Frosting

- 1/2 cup butter
- 1 8-oz. pkg. chocolate chips
- 1 8-oz. pkg. cream cheese
- 1 tablespoon vanilla
- 1 tablespoon instant coffee, or Pero coffee substitute
- Powdered sugar
- Nuts (optional)

1. Place butter and chocolate chips in microwave-proof dish and melt in microwave.
2. Place in food processor with cream cheese, vanilla, and coffee, (or Pero) and process until smooth.
3. Add powdered sugar and blend.
4. Add nuts, pulse, then spread on brownies.

Cookies & Crackers

Whole-Grain Graham Crackers

I love this graham cracker. It's not like the store-bought ones. Whether it's gluten free or not, the whole grain makes it amazing.
Try this for your next campfire s'more.

GF To make these fabulous graham crackers gluten free, use Gluten-Free WonderFlour™ and gluten-free oats.

Ingredients

6 1/2 cups Wonder-Flour™, or Gluten-Free WonderFlour™
1 1/2 cups rolled oats
1 cup coconut sugar
2 teaspoons salt
2 teaspoons baking soda
3 tablespoons ground cinnamon
3/4 cup organic agave, or 1 cup coconut sugar
1/2 cup coconut oil
2 sticks butter, room temperature
1 cup cold water

Yield: 4 dozen

Agave is great for baking. In cookies, it does add a cake-like texture, so I don't use it often unless I want that texture — for pumpkin cookies, for instance. If I want a crispy cookie, I use coconut sugar.

Directions

1 Preheat oven to 400°F.

2 In large bowl, whisk together dry ingredients.

3 Make a well in center of bowl.

4 In WonderMix bowl, with cookie whips, combine agave, oil, butter, and water. Mix well.

5 Replace whips with dough hook.

6 Add dry ingredients to mixture and mix until mixture forms a thick, crumbly/stiff dough.

7 Grease two 10" x 15" jelly roll pans.

8 Put half the dough on each sheet and press flat, using your fingers or a spatula.

9 Using a pizza cutter or butter knife, slice each sheet into 24 squares.

10 Bake for 13 to 18 minutes, or until lightly browned, rotating racks half-way through baking time if crackers appear to not be browning equally.

11 Remove pans from oven, place on wire racks, and allow cookies to cool on pans.

12 Re-slice or break apart, remove from pans, and store in airtight container or bag.

Hazelnut Multi-Grain Crackers

Ingredients

- 1 cup hazelnuts, about 4 1/2 oz., toasted and skinned
- 1 large egg, beaten
- 1/2 cup sorghum flour, freshly ground
- 1/2 cup whole buckwheat flour, freshly ground
- 1/3 cup Pecorino Pepato (peppered percorino cheese), freshly grated, or Romano cheese
- 1/2 teaspoon salt
- 2 tablespoons coconut sugar
- 5 tablespoons cold butter, cut into pieces
- 3 tablespoons heavy cream

Yield: 2 dozen

Directions

1. Preheat oven to 400°F.
2. In WonderMix blender, blend nuts and egg.
3. In WonderMix bowl, using cookie whips, blend flour, cheese, salt, sugar, and butter.
4. Add nut and egg mixture. Mix until it resembles coarse meal.
5. Replace whips with dough hook. Stir in cream until forms a dough.
6. Roll dough between two parchment papers.
7. Place on jelly roll pan and remove top parchment paper.
8. Score with knife and bake until golden brown.
9. Sprinkle with salt while still warm.

These crunchy crackers are absolutely amazing. Tender and delicious. You'll become addicted to them.

Sorghum and buckwheat are wonderful gluten-free grains. Freshly ground, they add an added boost of nutrition and flavor.

It's easy to toast and skin hazelnuts. Just spread hazelnuts in a single layer in baking pan and toast in the middle of oven for 10 to 15 minutes, until lightly colored and blistered. Wrap in kitchen towel and steam for about a minute. Rub nuts in towel, which will remove most of the skins, then cool.

Notes . . .

Whole-Grain Lavash Crackers

Lavash is a Middle Eastern cracker that is great served with hummus, other spreads, or just plain butter.

GF To make these crackers gluten free, use Gluten-Free Wonder-Flour™ instead of the Natural White or spelt flour.

Ingredients

- 3 cups spelt flour, freshly ground (adding whole-grain teff or amaranth to dough also works well)
- 1 teaspoon salt
- 1 teaspoon instant yeast
- 2 tablespoons sugar, or honey
- 2 tablespoons extra virgin olive oil
- 3/4 to 1 cup water
- Suggested toppings: Kosher salt, herbs, and seeds — sesame, poppy, chia, cumin, caraway, etc.
- 2 egg whites, for egg wash before baking

Yield: 3 dozen

Directions

1. In WonderMix bowl, with dough hook, place first 5 ingredients.
2. Add half the water and turn on mixer, adding additional water, if needed. The dough should pull away and form a nice ball.
3. Mix for 6 minutes then place in oiled bowl for 90 minutes to ferment.
4. After resting the dough, divide dough into 2 pieces.
5. Lightly spray counter and roll out dough as thin as possible.
6. Let rest, covering dough with moist cloth, if dough is too elastic.
7. Preheat oven to 350°F.
8. Roll out to desired thickness, the size of a jelly roll pan or cookie sheet.
9. Place on pan, lined with parchment paper.
10. Top with desired seeds or herbs.
11. Use a pizza cutter and cut dough into diamond shapes. Do not separate pieces; they will break apart after baking.
12. Bake until lightly browned, 15 to 20 minutes.
13. Remove from oven and let cool before breaking apart crackers.

Video: Hummus

Cookies & Crackers

Granola

Ingredients

12 cups old-fashioned rolled oats
2 cups amaranth, popped (see p. 73 for directions)
1/2 cup flax seed
2 cups pecans, chopped, or sliced almonds
1/2 cup pumpkin seeds
1 cup sunflower seeds
2 cups unsweetened coconut
1 cup dried cranberries
1 cup golden raisins
1 cup coconut oil
2 cups organic agave
1 cup coconut sugar
2 or 3 teaspoons vanilla
1 teaspoon nutmeg, freshly ground
1 teaspoon cinnamon
1 1/2 teaspoons salt
1 1/2 teaspoons maple flavoring

Yield: 5 quarts

Directions

1. Preheat oven to 335°F.
2. Combine first 9 ingredients.
3. In saucepan, heat coconut oil, agave, coconut sugar, vanilla, spices, salt, and maple flavoring.
4. Pour warm mixture over oat mixture and stir until moistened with liquid mixture.
5. Spray large pan with non-stick pan spray. Pour mixture in pan, spreading evenly. Do not over-fill.
6. Bake for 10 to 15 minutes, stirring every 3 minutes, until golden brown.
7. Remove and cool.
8. Store in airtight container for up to a month.

This granola is great for breakfast, snacks, or tossed on yogurt or ice cream. The plus side, it's the perfect nutrition for your body.

GF You can easily make this granola gluten free. Just be sure to use gluten-free oats.

Pumpkin Pancakes

These are delightful any time of the year but especially in the fall and winter months.

GF Use freshly ground Gluten-Free WonderFlour™ to add a boost of nutrition and flavor to these pancakes.

Ingredients

- 1 cup pumpkin, freshly cooked and pureed
- 6 eggs
- 2 cups buttermilk
- 2 teaspoons vanilla
- 1/4 cup canola oil
- 2-plus cups WonderFlour™, or spelt flour, freshly ground, or Gluten-Free WonderFlour™
- 1 teaspoon salt
- 1 tablespoon baking powder
- 1 teaspoon baking soda
- 1/2 teaspoon nutmeg
- 1/2 teaspoon cinnamon
- 1/4 teaspoon cardamom

Directions

1. Heat griddle.
2. In WonderMix, with French whips, whisk together pumpkin, eggs, buttermilk, vanilla, and oil.
3. Sift together dry ingredients.
4. Whisk together dry ingredients with wet ingredients. Add more flour if too runny.
5. Cook on hot griddle.
6. Top with Cranberry Buttermilk Syrup.

To cook pumpkin, cut in chunks and pressure cook for 6 minutes on high. Puree in your WonderMix Blender. Add water, if needed.

Cranberry Buttermilk Syrup

- 1 12-oz. bag cranberries
- 3 sticks butter
- 3 cups sugar
- 1 1/2 cups buttermilk
- 1 tablespoon vanilla
- 3 teaspoons baking soda

1. In deep, extra large saucepan, add cranberries, butter, sugar, and buttermilk.
2. Stir and bring to hard boil, letting cranberries burst.
3. Add vanilla and baking soda, and whisk thoroughly. It will bubble up and over quickly but it will calm down.
4. Remove from heat and serve warm with pancakes.

There are good salts and bad salts. Refined white salts have had all the minerals removed and have been processed to the point that our bodies do not know what they are. Good salts should have color and should not be harsh tasting. Unprocessed salts are good for the body in every way.

Whole-Grain Yogurt Pancakes

> Kefir works really well in this recipe. Kefir is a cultured yogurt-like beverage.

> Scan the QR Code below for link to a Chef Brad video on Gluten-Free Pancakes.

Ingredients

- 2 cups spelt flour, freshly ground, or your favorite flour, freshly ground
- 1/2 teaspoon salt
- 1 teaspoon baking soda
- 2 teaspoons baking powder
- 2 eggs
- 2 cups yogurt, or kefir
- 2 tablespoons organic agave
- 2 teaspoons vanilla
- 2 teaspoons butter, melted, or oil
- Topping: Fresh or freeze-dried berries and organic agave

Directions

1. Heat griddle.
2. In WonderMix, with French whips, place eggs, yogurt, agave, vanilla, and butter (or oil). Mix well.
3. Sift together dry ingredients.
4. Add dry ingredients to mixture. Mix quickly and don't continue mixing.
5. Scoop out on to hot griddle.
6. Sprinkle with freeze-dried berries.
7. Turn over when light brown.
8. Top with agave.

Video: Gluten-Free Pancakes

Pancakes & Waffles

Baked Berry Pancakes

Ingredients

- 4 tablespoons butter (divided)
- 1 cup milk
- 3 large eggs
- 1/2 teaspoon salt
- 2 teaspoons almond extract
- 1 teaspoon vanilla
- 3/4 cup coconut sugar, or raw sugar
- 1 cup WonderFlour™, Gluten-Free Wonder-Flour™ or other whole-grain flour, freshly ground on pastry setting
- 2 teaspoons baking powder
- 1 teaspoon baking soda
- 2 cups fresh berries

Directions

1. Preheat oven to 375 degrees.
2. Place 9-inch skillet or large pie pan in oven with 2 tablespoons of butter.
3. While that is heating up, mix pancakes.
4. In WonderMix bowl, with French whips, whisk together milk, eggs, salt, almond extract, and vanilla.
5. Add half the sugar and all the flour, baking powder, and baking soda.
6. Whisk well.
7. Remove pan from oven and pour batter in middle of pan. Let it fill pan.
8. Place fruit in center of pan and top with remaining sugar, leaving a 1-inch border around edge.
9. Place in oven and bake until edges are golden brown and puffed, 12 to 15 minutes.

This recipe works with any flour. Try different ones for a change in flavor and texture.

GF — Use gluten-free flour to make these pancakes gluten free.

Apple Blender Pancakes

Apple Blender Pancakes are wonderful and easy to make. I love to change the grains, and I usually add a whole apple to add nutrition and extra flavor. Try this recipe with any of the grains. They all work well.

To make this gluten free, use 1 cup sorghum instead of barley, and instead of oat groats, use 1 cup gluten-free oats, freshly ground. GF

Ingredients

2 1/2 cups milk
1 whole apple
1 cup pearled barley, or sorghum
1 cup oat groats
2 eggs, or equivalent of egg substitute
1/2 teaspoon salt
2 tablespoons cooking oil
1 teaspoon vanilla
1 teaspoon cinnamon
1 tablespoon baking powder

For lactose free, use soy milk or tofu drink mix for the liquid.

Directions

1. Heat griddle.
2. In WonderMix blender, combine milk, apple, barley (or sorghum), and oat groats.
3. Mix on high for 3 minutes.
4. Stop blender and add eggs, salt, oil, vanilla, and cinnamon.
5. Blend for 20 seconds.
6. Stop blender and add baking powder. Avoid over-whisking.
7. Pulse blender 3 times. Mixture will foam up and keep on growing.
8. Pour right away on to hot griddle.

Notes . . .

Video: Gluten-Free Pancakes

Kamut® Date Pancakes

Ingredients

- 1 cup loose dates
- 3 cups milk
- 3 cups Kamut® flour, freshly ground, or Gluten-Free WonderFlour™
- 1 ripe banana
- 1 teaspoon salt
- 1/3 cup cooking oil
- 1 tablespoon vanilla
- 1 cup sourdough starter, or 2 teaspoons instant yeast
- 2 tablespoons baking powder

Directions

1. Heat griddle.
2. In WonderMix blender, mix dates and milk.
3. Pour into WonderMix bowl, with French whips.
4. Add remaining ingredients and whisk well.
5. Once mixed, don't mix again.
6. Ladle on to hot griddle.

Whole grains that have not been processed and refined by man are complex carbohydrates, and they provide optimal nutrition for the body. Simple carbohydrates are processed foods that are devoid of nutrition, and they wreck havoc on the body.

I love a good pancake — one that tastes great and, at the same time, provides the body with goodness.

GF To make gluten free, simply use gluten-free flour, such as Gluten-Free WonderFlour™.

Almond Buttermilk Syrup

- 2 sticks butter
- 1 cup buttermilk
- 3 cups coconut sugar
- 2 teaspoons baking soda
- 2 teaspoons almond extract

1. Place butter, buttermilk, and sugar in deep, extra large pan, and bring to a boil.
2. Add soda and extract, and whisk well. Be careful; it will bubble up and over quickly. It will calm down, however, but it goes crazy in the beginning.

Notes . . .

Whole-Grain Crepes

I love crepes, and using whole grains really adds a nutty flavor. In my opinion, this really takes them over the top.

Don't be discouraged — the first crepe often does not work out.

Ingredients

- 6 whole eggs
- 1/4 cup coconut oil, melted
- Pinch salt
- 5 cups milk, or almond milk
- 1 cup buckwheat flour, freshly ground
- 2 cups spelt, freshly ground, or WonderFlour™ or Gluten-Free WonderFlour™
- 1 stick butter (to cover pan)

Directions

1. Heat crepe griddle.
2. In WonderMix blender, place all ingredients and mix very well.
3. Ladle or pour on to hot crepe griddle, which has been covered with butter. (I use an entire stick of butter to cover pan.)
4. Flip once, remove from crepe griddle, flip, and fill.

I have found that making the batter the night before makes a better crepe.

Notes . . .

Gluten-Free Crepes

Ingredients

- 6 whole eggs
- 1/4 cup coconut oil, melted, or butter
- 1 teaspoon vanilla, or almond extract
- Pinch salt
- 5 cups milk
- 1 cup buckwheat flour, freshly ground
- 2 cups whole-grain gluten-free flour, freshly ground
- Toppings: Unsweetened yogurt, fresh fruit (or caramelized apples or pears), organic agave, and whipped cream

Directions

In WonderMix blender, place all ingredients and mix very well.

To Cook Crepes:

1. Heat crepe griddle.
2. Coat pan or griddle with butter before pouring on crepe batter. (I use a whole stick of butter.)
3. Ladle or pour batter on to hot crepe griddle.
4. Flip once, remove from crepe griddle, flip, and fill.

To Fill:

1. Put a layer of unsweetened yogurt in a strip down middle of crepe.
2. Top with fresh fruit, or even caramelized apples or pears.
3. Add a drizzle of organic agave.
4. Top with whipped cream.
5. Fold it over and enjoy.

I don't worry if I have leftover batter. It only gets better when used later. I make the batter and leave it in the blender, and the next morning, I just mix it again.

Gluten-Free WonderFlour™ is a blend of gluten-free grains, and when freshly ground, provides optimal nutrition and flavor.

Notes . . .

Sourdough Buttermilk Waffles

These waffles are tender and amazing. Don't worry if you don't use all the batter; leftover batter makes even better waffles.

Ingredients

- 5 cups spelt flour, freshly ground on pastry setting
- 5 cups buttermilk
- 1/4 cup organic agave
- 1/4 cup butter, melted
- 1 cup sourdough starter
- 6 large eggs
- 2 teaspoons sea salt
- 2 teaspoons baking soda
- 2 teaspoons vanilla

Directions

1. The night before serving, begin waffle batter. In large bowl or container with lid, place spelt flour, buttermilk, agave, melted butter, and sourdough starter.
2. Whisk well and cover.
3. Leave on counter overnight.
4. When ready to serve, spray waffle iron with non-stick pan spray and heat up.
5. In WonderMix, with French whips, whisk together eggs, salt, baking soda, and vanilla.
6. Add batter and whisk until evenly incorporated.
7. Ladle on to hot waffle iron.
8. If you have leftover batter, place in refrigerator until ready to use. Remove from refrigerator. Whisk well and use.

Video: Buttermilk Waffles

Gluten-Free Yeasted Buttermilk Waffles

Ingredients

- 1 tablespoon instant yeast
- 3 tablespoons coconut sugar, or organic agave
- 5 cups buttermilk
- 1/2 cup butter, melted
- 2 teaspoons salt
- 5 cups gluten-free flour blend
- 5 eggs, beaten
- 1 1/2 teaspoons baking soda
- 1 tablespoon vanilla

For a Tender Waffle: Cook on lower temperature.
For a Crisp Waffle: Cook on higher temperature.
To Serve All at Once: Place cooked waffles in oven pre-heated to 200°.
To Store Waffles: Cool on wire rack and place in plastic freezer bags. Freeze up to one month.

Directions

1. The night before serving, begin waffle batter. In large bowl or container with lid, place yeast, sugar, buttermilk, butter, salt, and flour.
2. Whisk well and cover.
3. Leave on counter overnight.
4. When ready to serve, spray waffle iron with non-stick pan spray and heat up.
5. In WonderMix, with French whips, beat eggs, then add baking soda and vanilla.
6. Add batter and whisk until evenly incorporated.
7. Ladle on to hot waffle iron.

Healthy waffles are the perfect way to start your day.

Whenever possible, use freshly ground gluten-free flour.

Video: Gluten-Free Waffle Sandwiches

Brown Rice Waffles

Ingredients

- 4 eggs
- 1/4 cup butter, melted
- 2 cups buttermilk
- 1 cup long-grain brown rice, cooked and chilled
- 1/4 cup organic agave
- 1 teaspoon vanilla
- Pinch of salt
- 2 cups brown rice, freshly ground
- 1 tablespoon baking powder

Directions

1. Heat waffle iron.
2. In WonderMix bowl, with French whips, all the ingredients except baking powder. Whisk well.
3. Add baking powder. Whisk well and quickly. Don't whisk again.
4. Spray waffle iron with non-stick pan spray, or brush with melted butter.
5. Ladle batter on to hot waffle iron.
6. Cook to desired brownness.

Rice flour does not hold up well in pancakes, but for waffles, it's amazing. The waffle iron allows for it to hold together. Packed with goodness and flavor, these waffles are a crowd pleaser. The brown rice leaves the outside of the waffle crispy and light.

Brown rice is gluten free and is terrific in these waffles.

When adding baking powder to pancakes — and especially waffles — avoid over-whisking.

Notes …

Video: Smoked Pork Waffles

Master Muffin Recipe

Muffins should be light and tender. The less you work the batter, the better the muffin. Muffins are a great way to start the day — that is, if you add high-fiber ingredients.

Muffins **GF** are easy to make gluten free. Simply use Gluten-Free WonderFlour™ or other gluten-free flour.

Ingredients

2 sticks butter
2 cups sugar
4 eggs
7 cups WonderFlour™, or Gluten-Free WonderFlour™
2 tablespoons baking powder
1 teaspoon baking soda
1 teaspoon salt
3 cups buttermilk

Yield: 2 dozen

Options:
Add:
Cooked grains
Nuts
Flax meal
Fruits
Grated vegetables

Directions

1. Preheat oven to 375°F.
2. In WonderMix bowl, with French whips, cream together butter and sugar.
3. After light and fluffy, add eggs, one at a time.
4. In separate bowl, sift together dry ingredients.
5. Replace whips with dough hook.
6. Add dry ingredients, alternating with buttermilk. It is important to mix lightly.
7. Spoon into greased muffin tin and bake for 25 to 30 minutes, or until golden brown.

Let me be clear . . . the muffins they sell out there are not muffins; they are cake in muffin papers and shapes. They are full of white sugar and white flour, with nothing good to offer the body. A muffin should be slightly sweet, filled with flavor, and good for you.

Notes . . .

Morning Glory Muffins

Ingredients

- 4 cups spelt flour, or any whole-grain flours, freshly ground
- 3 teaspoons baking soda
- 1 tablespoon baking powder
- 1 tablespoon cinnamon
- 1 teaspoon salt
- 6 eggs
- 1 cup red quinoa, cooked
- 1 cup organic agave
- 1 cup raisins, plumped with hot water
- 4 cups carrots, grated
- 2 cups apples, grated
- 1 cup almonds, sliced
- 2 cups unsweetened coconut
- 1 tablespoon vanilla
- 1 2/3 cups cooking oil, or coconut oil

Yield: 3 dozen

Directions

1. Preheat oven to 350°F.
2. In WonderMix, with dough hook, combine all dry ingredients.
3. In large bowl, whip eggs then add remaining ingredients.
4. Add wet ingredients to dry ingredients, and mix. Do not over-mix. Muffins are better if mixed lightly.
5. Bake for 25 minutes.

Notes . . .

This muffin is full of flavor and goodness. Muffins should not resemble cake, sickenly sweet and devoid of nutrition. A muffin should be tender and delightful — a culinary expression.

GF For optimal nutrition and flavor, use freshly ground gluten-free flour.

To plump raisins, put them in a bowl and cover them with boiling water. After 10 minutes, strain, throwing away the water. The raisins will be nice and plump.

Zucchini Muffins

These muffins are so tender and so good for you.

GF To make these muffins gluten free, just use a gluten-free flour.

Ingredients

- 4 eggs
- 2 cups organic agave
- 1 cup coconut oil
- 2 teaspoons vanilla
- 4 1/4 cups zucchini, shredded
- 3 to 5 cups flour blend, freshly ground
- 2 teaspoons baking powder
- 1 1/4 teaspoons salt
- 2 teaspoons baking soda
- 1 1/3 tablespoons cinnamon
- 1 1/3 cups almonds, pecans, walnuts, or other nuts (optional)
- 1 1/3 cups raisins (optional)

Yield: 2 dozen

Directions

1. Preheat oven to 350°F.
2. In WonderMix bowl, with French whips, mix first 4 ingredients to a mayonnaise-like texture.
3. Replace whips with dough hook. Add remaining ingredients. Do not over-mix.
4. Place in muffin tins sprayed with non-stick pan spray.
5. Bake for 20 minutes.

Notes . . .

Muffins & Biscuits

Sourdough English Muffins

When you can make English muffins this good at home, why would you want to buy them at the store?

Ingredients

- 2 cups sourdough starter
- 3/4 cup buttermilk
- 2 3/4 to 3 cups spelt flour, freshly ground and sifted
- 6 tablespoons popcorn, freshly ground
- 2 teaspoons baking soda
- 1/4 teaspoon salt

Yield: 2 dozen

Directions

1. In WonderMix, with dough hook, mix sourdough starter and buttermilk.
2. Combine flour, 4 tablespoons of the cornmeal, soda, and salt. Add to buttermilk mixture.
3. Stir to combine, adjusting flour, if needed. Dough should be sticky.
4. Mix for 5 minutes.
5. Remove from mixer and place in lightly oiled bowl.
6. Let rest for one hour.
7. Turn on to lightly floured surface.
8. Knead until smooth, adding more flour, if necessary.
9. Roll dough to 2/3-inch thickness.
10. Cover and let rise a few minutes.
11. Using 3-inch cutter, cut muffins.
12. Sprinkle sheet of parchment paper with remaining cornmeal.
13. Cover and let rise until very light, about 45 minutes.
14. Heat a griddle to medium high heat. When griddle is hot, gently place muffins on griddle and bake on both sides until golden brown.

Notes . . .

Gluten-Free English Muffins

Ingredients

- 1 1/2 cups warm water
- 1/2 cup potato starch
- 5 eggs
- 1/3 cup organic agave
- 1 tablespoon salt
- 1/4 cup coconut oil
- 4 teaspoons xanthan gum
- 3 tablespoons instant yeast
- 1 cup quinoa, cooked
- 1/2 cup popcorn, freshly ground
- 4 cups Gluten-Free WonderFlour™

Yield: 2 dozen

Directions

1. In WonderMix bowl, with dough hook, place ingredients and mix well. Dough should be more like heavy cake batter rather than bread dough.
2. Mix well for 6 minutes.
3. Scoop spoon of dough into gluten-free flour and roll.
4. Place on parchment and press down into circle.
5. Let rise to double, while preheating oven to 400°F.
6. Put in oven, immediately reducing temperature to 350°F, and bake for 20 minutes, or until golden brown.

Perfect for your Sunday morning Eggs Benedict. So tender and delightful.

Use a blend of three or more gluten-free grains.

Also works for sandwich bread and flatbread.

Video: Gluten-Free All-Purpose Dough

Yeasted Buttermilk Biscuits

Adding yeast to a biscuit really enhances the texture and flavor.

Natural White flour, produced by Wheat Montana, is an all-purpose flour that is unbleached and unbromated, which means it is free of potassium bromate, a toxin found in many commercial flours.

Ingredients

- 1 tablespoon instant yeast
- 1/4 cup warm water
- 1 tablespoon sugar
- 2 cups Natural White flour
- 1 teaspoon baking soda
- 1 tablespoon baking powder
- 2 teaspoons salt
- 1/4 cup coconut sugar
- 1 1/2 sticks butter, cut in 1/2-inch pieces chilled
- 1 1/2 cups buttermilk, room temperature
- 3 cups spelt flour, freshly ground

Yield: 2 dozen

Directions

1. In separate bowl, mix yeast, water, and sugar.
2. Let rest for 5 to 10 minutes.
3. In WonderMix bowl, with French whips, add flour, baking soda, baking powder, salt, coconut sugar, and chopped, chilled butter.
4. Turn on mixer and cut in butter. You want the butter to be pea size. Do not over-mix.
5. Replace whips with dough hook.
6. Add yeast mixture and half the buttermilk.
7. Turn on mixer, adding more buttermilk. You want a really moist and sticky dough. Do not over-mix.
8. Place lid on mixer and let rise, 10 to 15 minutes.
9. While biscuits are rising, preheat oven to 400°F.
10. Remove dough from mixer and place on floured surface.
11. Gently knead.
12. Roll out dough and cut with biscuit cutter.
13. Place biscuits close together on baking pan.
14. Bake for 12 to 15 minutes, or until biscuits are golden brown.

Gluten-Free Yeasted Buttermilk Biscuits

Ingredients

- 1 tablespoon instant yeast
- 1/4 cup warm water
- 1 tablespoon sugar
- 1/2 cup potato flour
- 5 cups gluten-free flour blend
- 1 teaspoon baking soda
- 1 tablespoon baking powder
- 2 teaspoons salt
- 1/4 cup coconut sugar
- 1 1/2 sticks butter, cut in 1/2-inch pieces, chilled
- 1 1/2 cups buttermilk, room temperature

Yield: 2 dozen

Directions

1. In separate bowl, mix yeast, water, and sugar. Let rest for 5 to 10 minutes.
2. In WonderMix bowl, with French whips, add flour, baking soda, baking powder, salt, sugar, and chopped, chilled butter.
3. Turn on mixer and cut in butter into flour (pea size). Don't over-mix.
4. Replace whips with dough hook. Add yeast mixture and half the buttermilk.
5. Turn on mixer and mix, adding more buttermilk. You want a really moist and sticky dough. Once again, do not over-mix.
6. Place lid on mixer and let rise, while preheating oven to 400°F.
7. Later remove from mixer, place on floured surface, and gently knead.
8. Roll out dough and cut with biscuit cutter. Place close together on baking pan.
9. Bake for 12 to 15 minutes, or until biscuits are golden brown.

Adding yeast to a biscuit really enhances the texture and flavor.

Use a blend of three or more gluten-free grains, freshly ground.

I love adding whole-grain teff to my biscuits. I love the texture it gives biscuits. Teff should be a standard in your pantry. Try adding 1/2 cup of teff to the recipe and see how you like it.

Video: Gluten-Free Gravy

Muffins & Biscuits

Sourdough Buttermilk Biscuits

Nothing like a good, tender biscuit, topped with jam and butter.

Ingredients

- 1 cup flour
- 1 cup sourdough starter
- 1 cup milk
- 1/4 cup raw sugar
- 3 1/2 cups flour
- 4 teaspoons baking soda
- 2 teaspoons baking powder
- 1 teaspoon salt
- 1 cup shortening, or butter

Yield: 2 dozen

Directions

1. Measure first 4 ingredients into a non-metallic bowl and beat until smooth.
2. Cover loosely with damp cloth and let stand in a warm place for 8 to 18 hours (the longer it stands, the stronger the flavor gets).
3. Preheat oven to 450°F.
4. Stir down batter.
5. In WonderMix bowl, with French whips, add remaining dry ingredients.
6. Cut in shortening (or butter).
7. Replace whips with dough hook. Blend in first mixture and turn out on to lightly floured surface.
8. Add more flour, if necessary, to make soft dough.
9. Roll out 1/2 inch thick and cut with floured glass or biscuit cutter, and place on an ungreased cookie sheet.
10. Bake for 12 minutes.

GF Sourdough Buttermilk Biscuits

Ingredients

- 1 cup gluten-free flour
- 1 tablespoon instant yeast
- 1/2 cup warm water
- 1 cup buttermilk
- 1/4 cup raw sugar
- 4 cups Gluten-Free WonderFlour™
- 4 teaspoons baking soda
- 2 teaspoons baking powder
- 1 teaspoon salt
- 1 cup shortening, or butter

Yield: 2 dozen

Directions

1. In WonderMix bowl, with French whips, add first 5 ingredients. Beat until smooth.
2. Cover loosely with damp towel or cloth. Let stand in a warm place 8 to 18 hours.
3. Preheat oven to 450°F.
4. Stir down batter.
5. In another bowl, mix remaining dry ingredients.
6. Replace whips with dough hook. Cut in shortening (or butter) until mixture looks like coarse crumbs.
7. Blend in first mixture and turn out on to lightly floured surface. Add more flour, if necessary, to make a soft dough.
8. Roll out 1/2-inch thick and cut with floured glass or biscuit cutter, and place on ungreased cookie sheet.
9. Bake for 12 minutes.

The longer the sourdough is allowed to stand, the stronger the flavor gets.

Biscuits and gravy go together perfectly. Gluten-Free Wonder-Flour™ is great for making gravies. Actually, it makes the gravy tastes better — and you have the added bonus of all the fiber and goodness of the grains. Just use your regular gravy recipes, substituting freshly-ground gluten-free flours.

Video: Gluten-Free Gravy

Sweet Potato Spelt Biscuits

Ingredients

- 4 cups spelt flour, freshly ground on pastry setting
- 1 tablespoon baking powder
- 1 teaspoon salt
- 12 tablespoons butter, chilled
- 2 cups sweet potatoes, cooked and mashed, or riced
- 1/2 to 3/4 cup heavy cream, or buttermilk

Yield: 2 dozen

Directions

1. Preheat oven to 400°F.
2. In WonderMix bowl, with French whips, add dry ingredients and mix.
3. Cut in butter until the size of peas.
4. Replace whips with dough hook.
5. Add sweet potatoes and cream. Mix until lightly mixed.
6. Remove from bowl and place on floured board.
7. Roll out dough and cut biscuits.
8. Place close together on cookie sheet.
9. Bake until browned, about 10 to 12 minutes.

These are the most tender, dearest biscuits I've ever eaten.

GF To make these biscuits gluten free, use Gluten-Free WonderFlour™ and add 1/2 cup potato starch to the recipe.

When you take the white flour out of biscuits, it does change them, and when you don't have all the over-processed ingredients often used, the biscuits are likewise different. I love whole-grain biscuits. They are tender and delicate, depending on the grains used. Try different blends of grains until you find one that is perfect for you.

Notes . . .

Buttermilk Pastry Dough

This recipe will yield two 9- or 10-inch pie shells.

Ingredients

- 2 sticks frozen butter
- 3 cups spelt flour, freshly ground on pastry setting
- 3 tablespoons sugar
- 1 teaspoon salt
- 1/2 to 2/3 cup buttermilk

Yield: 2 shells

Directions

1. Grate butter into chilled bowl.
2. In WonderMix bowl, using dough hook, place flour, sugar, and salt.
3. Mix well then add grated butter and mix lightly.
4. Add buttermilk until dough forms.
5. Remove from bowl and divide into 2 pieces.
6. Roll out.
7. This dough can be stored in refrigerator or freezer.

For cream pie, bake pie shell in 350°F oven for 20 to 25 minutes. Remove, cool, and fill. For other pies, bake as instructed.

Video: Flaky Pie Crust

Muffins & Biscuits 117

Gluten-Free Pastry Dough

Ingredients

- 2 sticks frozen butter
- 3 cups Gluten-Free WonderFlour™, freshly ground on pastry setting
- 3 tablespoons sugar
- 1 teaspoon salt
- 1/2 to 2/3 cup heavy cream

Yield: 2 shells

Directions

1. Grate butter into a chilled bowl.
2. In WonderMix bowl, using French whips, place flour, sugar, and salt.
3. Mix well.
4. Replace whips with dough hook.
5. Add grated butter and mix lightly.
6. Add heavy cream until dough forms.
7. Remove from bowl and divide into 2 pieces.
8. This dough is best pressed in pie pan.
9. This dough can be stored in the refrigerator or freezer.
10. For cream pie, bake pie shell in 350°F oven for 20 to 25 minutes. Remove and let cool. Fill with cream filling. For other pies, bake as instructed.

If you're gluten free, there's no reason to deprive yourself of a good, flaky pastry shell.

Grains offer fiber, which is essential for health and wellness. We need more fiber in our diets to keep our bodies healthy and fit. Whole grains are packed with fiber, as well as minerals and essential oils.

Making a gluten-free pie crust involves pressing, rather than rolling out. It's difficult to make a gluten-free pie crust top but this recipe is great for open pies — cream pies, pumpkin pies, and quiche. For baked pies, press dough out, fill, and bake. For cream pies and the like, press dough out, bake, and fill.

Remember, this is a pressed dough. Be creative in topping your gluten-free fruit pies. After pressing out the dough, you can cut out shapes, using cookie cutters, then with a spatula gently lift and place cut-out pieces on the pie surface for a unique top crust.

Notes . . .

Video: Buttermilk Pie

Popovers

Popovers are meant to be eaten immediately, so plan your meal accordingly.

Ingredients

2 1/2 cups spelt flour, freshly ground
1/2 teaspoon salt
6 large eggs
2 1/2 cups milk
2 tablespoon unsalted butter, melted
2 tablespoons unsalted butter, cut into 12 even pieces

Yield: 1 dozen

Directions

1. Set rack in middle of oven and preheat to 400°F.
2. In WonderMix blender, blend flour, salt, eggs, milk, and melted butter until mixture is the consistency of heavy cream, about 1 to 2 minutes.
3. Batter can be stored in the refrigerator but should be used at room temperature.
4. Oil or spray popover pan. Preheat pan in oven about 2 minutes.
5. Place 1 small piece of butter in each cup and place back in preheated oven until butter is bubbling, about 1 minute.
6. Fill each cup half full with melted butter.
7. Bake 20 minutes, then reduce temperature to 300°F and continue baking 20 more minutes.
8. Makes 12 to 24 popovers, depending on size of pan.

Variation:

Fill each cup with 1 tablespoon Parmesan cheese, in addition to the butter. Add batter until cup is half full.

Notes . . .

Gluten-Free Savory Popovers

Ingredients

- 2 1/2 cups Gluten-Free WonderFlour™, freshly ground
- 1/3 cup potato starch
- 1/2 teaspoon salt
- 6 large eggs
- 2 1/2 cups milk
- 2 teaspoons baking powder
- 2 teaspoons pepper, freshly ground
- 2 tablespoons unsalted butter, cut into 12 even pieces
- 2 tablespoons unsalted butter, melted
- 1 tablespoon fresh rosemary, finely chopped
- Parmesan cheese

Yield: 1 dozen

Variation:
Fill each popover cup with 1 tablespoon of Parmesan cheese, in addition to the butter. Add batter until cup is half full.

Directions

1. Set rack in middle of oven and preheat oven to 400°F.
2. In WonderMix blender, blend first 7 ingredients until mixture is consistency of heavy cream, about 1 to 2 minutes.
3. Batter can be stored in the refrigerator but should be used at room temperature.
4. Oil or spray popover pan. Preheat pan in oven about 2 minutes.
5. Place 1 small piece of butter in each cup and place back in preheated oven until butter is bubbling, about 1 minute.
6. Fill each cup half full with butter. Top with fresh rosemary and Parmesan cheese.
7. Bake 20 minutes, then reduce temperature to 300°F and continue baking 20 more minutes.
8. Makes 12 to 24 popovers, depending on size of pan.

These almost resemble popovers. The main reason I added this recipe, however, is because it makes the most wonderful dinner rolls ever.

Using Gluten-Free WonderFlour™ ups the nutrition in any recipe.

Notes . . .

Polish Stoneware

I have been collecting Polish stoneware for almost 20 years. I love it so much. Not only do I love the colors but how durable it is. My first pieces still look brand new. They are non-stick, oven-proof, microwave-proof, and suitable for the freezer. This stoneware is free of harmful chemicals, such as lead and cadmium.

I have to say, dishes are one of my things, but I hate it when I spend money on them and then they chip or break easily. Over the last twenty years, I have had only one piece in my Polish stoneware collection crack and that was a coffee mug. That says a lot, considering how many pieces I have and how much I use them.

I am so excited to feature this amazing stoneware in this cookbook. It is beautiful and so functional. There are elaborate designs to suit every kitchen and personal preference.

I hope you enjoy the photographs of these fabulous everyday baked goods baked in beautiful Polish stoneware as much as we enjoyed taking them!

Chef Brad

"America's Grain Guy"

Index

Breads

Basic Whole-Wheat Bread 4
Whole-Grain Gluten-Free Bread 7
Whole-Wheat Flax Sourdough Bread 8
Gluten-Free Flax Bread 9
Buckwheat Rustic Bread 10
Flax Seed Rustic Bread 12
Gluten-Free Rustic Flat Bread 13
Red Rice Chia Bread 14
Gluten-Free Red Rice Chia Bread 17
Multi-Grain Focaccia Bread 18
Gluten-Free Rosemary Focaccia Bread 21
Teff Pizza Dough 22
Gluten-Free Pizza Dough 25
Flax Dinner Rolls 26
Gluten-Free Dinner Rolls 29
Burger Buns 30
Gluten-Free Burger Buns 33
Banana Bread Plus 34
Old-Fashioned Cornbread 37
Cinnamon Rolls 38
Gluten-Free Cinnamon Rolls 41
Zucchini Loaves 42
Bread Pudding 44
Whole-Grain Croutons 45

Cakes

Gluten-Free Almond Butter Cake 46
Fresh Apple Cake 48
Spelt Pickled Lemon Bread 51
Short Cake 53
Spelt Chocolate Cupcakes 54
Carrot Cake 56
Whole-Grain Walnut Bundt Cake 59
Yellow Lemon Cake 60

Cookies & Crackers

Whole-Grain Chocolate Chip Cookies 63
Whole-Grain Oatmeal Cookies 64
Italian Cornmeal Cookies 65
Basil Spice Cookies 66
Red Quinoa Coconut Cookies 67
Whole-Grain Pecan Bars 69
Bacon Toffee Cookies 70
Spelt Buttermilk Cookies 71
Amaranth Cookies 73
Peanut Butter Cookies 74
Whole-Grain Toffee Cookies 76
Basil Brownies 79
Whole-Grain Graham Crackers 80

Hazelnut Multi-Grain Crackers 83
Whole-Grain Lavash Crackers 84
Granola 85

Pancakes & Waffles

Pumpkin Pancakes 86
Whole-Grain Yogurt Pancakes 88
Baked Berry Pancakes 89
Apple Blender Pancakes 90
Kamut® Date Pancakes 93
Whole-Grain Crepes 94
Gluten-Free Crepes 97
Sourdough Buttermilk Waffles 98
Gluten-Free Yeasted Buttermilk Waffles 99
Brown Rice Waffles 101

Muffins & Biscuits

Master Muffin Recipe 102
Morning Glory Muffins 105
Zucchini Muffins 106
Sourdough English Muffins 108
Gluten-Free English Muffins 109
Yeasted Buttermilk Biscuits 110
Gluten-Free Yeasted Buttermilk Biscuits 111
Sourdough Buttermilk Biscuits 112
GF Sourdough Buttermilk Biscuits 113
Sweet Potato Spelt Biscuits 115

Buttermilk Pastry Dough 116
Gluten-Free Pastry Dough 117
Popovers 118
Gluten-Free Savory Popovers 121

Notes . . .

Ongoing Education
Additional Cooking Videos by Chef Brad

Quality Equipment for Quality Baking

For the serious baker, gluten free or not, and for those who care about eating good foods made at home, a good mixer and mill are essential. I personally love the WonderMix and WonderMill. Mixing and grinding grains have never been easier and faster.

The WonderMix is a powerful, easy-to-use machine. It takes up little space on the counter and actually brings joy into the kitchen.

A good mill is a lifesaver. You can grind grains fresh, ensuring optimal freshness and nutrition. Any and all of the grains grind well, producing pastry flour to bread flour, on the WonderMill — the fastest, cleanest, and quietest mill on the market today.

With both of these pieces of equipment, your baking will reach higher levels of quality and goodness.

Made in the USA
San Bernardino, CA
06 August 2017